CEOE 128 Blind/Visual Impairment

Iris Q. McKinley

This page is intentionally left blank.

This page is intentionally left blank.

Table of Content

This page is intentionally left blank.

Chapter 1 – Questions

QUESTION 1

Which of the following physical characteristics is typically observed in visually impaired students during adolescence?

- A. Enhanced peripheral vision
- B. Slower gross motor skill development
- C. Improved visual acuity
- D. Rapid height growth spurt

Answer:

QUESTION 2

How might a visually impaired adolescent's communicative development be affected by their condition?

- A. Enhanced speech articulation
- B. Delayed language acquisition
- C. Increased nonverbal communication skills
- D. Quicker vocabulary expansion

Answer:

QUESTION 3

What cognitive challenge might visually impaired adolescents commonly face in their development?

- A. Enhanced spatial reasoning skills
- B. Difficulty with abstract thinking
- C. Faster memory retention
- D. Improved attention span

Answer:

QUESTION 4

How might the psychological development of visually impaired adolescents differ from that of their sighted peers?

- A. Increased social anxiety
- B. Lower self-esteem
- C. Enhanced self-confidence
- D. Greater risk of depression

Answer:

QUESTION 5

Which factor related to cultural and language differences could impact the social/emotional development of visually impaired students?

    A. Familiarity with braille in different cultures
    B. Uniformity of social norms across cultures
    C. Similarity in emotional expression across cultures
    D. Consistency in language development milestones

Answer:

QUESTION 6

Which part of the visual system is primarily responsible for perceiving color and fine details in the visual field?

    A. Cornea
    B. Retina
    C. Optic nerve
    D. Lens

Answer:

QUESTION 7

In typically developing children, which visual milestone typically occurs first during infancy?

    A. Tracking moving objects with their eyes
    B. Recognizing and responding to faces
    C. Focusing on objects at different distances
    D. Differentiating between colors

Answer:

QUESTION 8

Which structure in the eye helps to control the amount of light that enters the eye and contributes to focusing on near and distant objects?

    A. Cornea
    B. Retina
    C. Optic nerve
    D. Iris

Answer:

QUESTION 9

During which stage of visual development in children do they typically refine their ability to perceive and differentiate between colors?

    A. Infancy
    B. Early childhood
    C. Middle childhood
    D. Adolescence

Answer:

QUESTION 10

Which component of the visual system is responsible for transmitting visual information from the retina to the brain for further processing?

    A. Cornea
    B. Lens
    C. Optic nerve
    D. Vitreous humor

Answer:

QUESTION 11

What is the significance of visual experiences during early childhood for children with visual impairments?

    A. Early visual experiences have minimal impact on their development.
    B. Visual experiences can compensate for other sensory deficits.
    C. Visual experiences help establish cognitive foundations.
    D. Visual experiences primarily influence physical development.

Answer:

QUESTION 12

Which part of the eye focuses light onto the retina to create a clear image?

    A. Cornea
    B. Lens
    C. Optic nerve
    D. Sclera

Answer:

QUESTION 13

In the context of common effects of visual impairments on cognitive development, which of the following is a potential challenge that a visually impaired child may encounter in a classroom setting?

    A. Enhanced ability to visualize complex concepts
    B. Difficulty with spatial orientation and navigation
    C. Faster rate of information processing
    D. Improved reading comprehension skills

Answer:

QUESTION 14

How might a visual impairment impact a child's language development?

    A. Accelerated vocabulary acquisition
    B. Reduced exposure to visual stimuli
    C. Enhanced phonological awareness
    D. Improved reading fluency

Answer:

QUESTION 15

In a case study scenario, a visually impaired student is struggling with understanding abstract concepts in mathematics. What educational strategies could be beneficial to address this challenge?

    A. Emphasizing visual aids for abstract concepts
    B. Incorporating tactile materials and hands-on activities
    C. Increasing screen time for digital learning
    D. Providing more written assignments

Answer:

QUESTION 16

How might a visual impairment affect a child's cognitive development in the area of problem-solving skills?

    A. Enhanced problem-solving abilities due to increased focus
    B. Delayed development of spatial reasoning
    C. Faster processing of visual information
    D. Improved memory retention

Answer:

QUESTION 17

What role can assistive technology play in supporting the language development of visually impaired students?

    A. Minimizing the need for verbal communication
    B. Promoting dependency on auditory input
    C. Providing access to text-to-speech software and Braille displays
    D. Reducing the need for speech therapy

Answer:

QUESTION 18

In a hypothetical scenario, a visually impaired student is struggling to participate in group discussions. What strategies can a special education teacher employ to facilitate their active participation?

    A. Assigning more individual tasks to avoid group discussions
    B. Encouraging the student to sit at the back of the classroom
    C. Providing auditory cues and facilitating turn-taking
    D. Ignoring the student's participation to avoid singling them out

Answer:

QUESTION 19

How might a visual impairment affect a child's cognitive development related to memory and recall?

    A. Enhanced memory retention due to heightened focus
    B. Improved ability to process visual information
    C. Potential challenges with visual memory tasks
    D. Accelerated development of working memory

Answer:

QUESTION 20

Which type of assessment is most appropriate for evaluating the specific reading and writing needs of a visually impaired student?

- A. Visual assessments
- B. Auditory assessments
- C. Braille assessments
- D. Kinesthetic assessments

Answer:

QUESTION 21

In a case study scenario, a visually impaired student has been struggling in a mainstream classroom setting. Which assessment information would be most crucial for making appropriate placement and program recommendations?

- A. Results of a general cognitive assessment
- B. Teacher observations of the student's behavior
- C. Functional vision assessment results
- D. Parental input on the student's preferences

Answer:

QUESTION 22

How can assessment information be effectively used to monitor the progress of a visually impaired student over time?

- A. Relying solely on standardized test scores
- B. Comparing the student's performance to sighted peers
- C. Setting specific, measurable goals and tracking achievements
- D. Conducting assessments less frequently to reduce stress

Answer:

QUESTION 23

In the context of assessing visually impaired students, what is a primary goal of assessment when identifying students with special needs?

- A. Identifying students who require glasses or visual aids
- B. Identifying students with social communication disorders
- C. Determining the degree of visual impairment and its impact
- D. Identifying students with high IQ scores

Answer:

QUESTION 24

In a hypothetical scenario, a visually impaired student is struggling with mathematics but excelling in language arts. What type of assessment might be particularly helpful in making placement decisions for this student?

- A. General aptitude assessment
- B. Curriculum-based assessment
- C. Vision-related assessment
- D. Parental naire

Answer:

QUESTION 25

Which assessment approach is most effective in evaluating a visually impaired student's compensatory skills, such as orientation and mobility?

    A. Paper-and-pencil assessments
    B. Observational assessments
    C. Parent interviews
    D. General health assessments

Answer:

QUESTION 26

When determining the degree of need in compensatory skills areas for a visually impaired student, which assessment information should be prioritized?

    A. Results of standardized academic tests
    B. Assessment of social skills
    C. Evaluation of adaptive technology proficiency
    D. Assessment of daily living skills and independence

Answer:

QUESTION 27

In assessing daily living and functional life skills of visually impaired students, which assessment approach is most likely to provide comprehensive information?

    A. A standardized written test
    B. Observational assessment in real-life situations
    C. Parent interviews
    D. Teacher reports

Answer:

QUESTION 28

A visually impaired student is experiencing difficulties with fine motor skills. Which assessment tool would be most appropriate to identify specific motor skill deficits?

    A. A general cognitive assessment
    B. A vision-related assessment
    C. A fine motor skills assessment
    D. A speech and language assessment

Answer:

QUESTION 29

In assessing the communicative competence of a visually impaired student, what should a special education teacher consider to be the primary goal of the assessment?

A. Identifying the student's primary mode of communication
B. Assessing the student's ability to use written language
C. Determining the student's level of visual acuity
D. Evaluating the student's general cognitive abilities

Answer:

QUESTION 30

A visually impaired student has undergone multiple assessments, and the results appear inconsistent. What is the first step a special education teacher should take when faced with such a situation?

A. Disregard the inconsistent results and rely on teacher observations.
B. Consult with other professionals, such as a school psychologist or speech therapist.
C. Re-administer the assessments to ensure accuracy.
D. Share the results directly with the student without interpretation.

Answer:

QUESTION 31

In a case study scenario, a visually impaired student is struggling with daily living skills such as cooking and personal hygiene. What type of assessment would be most valuable in this situation?

A. Visual acuity assessment
B. Occupational therapy assessment
C. Speech and language assessment
D. General cognitive assessment

Answer:

QUESTION 32

Why is ongoing assessment particularly important for visually impaired students?

A. It allows for tracking changes in visual acuity.
B. It helps identify changes in communication preferences.
C. It facilitates adjustments to individualized support and interventions.
D. It reduces the need for formal assessments.

Answer:

QUESTION 33

When communicating assessment results to the parents of a visually impaired student, what should be the primary focus?

A. Highlighting the student's academic achievements
B. Providing a detailed overview of the assessment process
C. Emphasizing the student's strengths and areas for improvement
D. Recommending a change in educational placement

Answer:

QUESTION 34

Sarah, a visually impaired student, has recently joined your inclusive classroom. You've noticed that she often struggles to navigate her way around the classroom and frequently bumps into objects. What assessment would you prioritize to address this issue?

A. Visual acuity assessment
B. Orientation and mobility assessment
C. Speech and language assessment
D. General cognitive assessment

Answer:

QUESTION 35

Mark, a visually impaired student, is struggling with reading and writing tasks. His teacher suspects that he may have specific difficulties related to his visual impairment. What assessment approach would be most effective in identifying his specific needs?

A. A standardized reading comprehension test
B. A general cognitive assessment
C. A functional vision assessment
D. A speech and language assessment

Answer:

QUESTION 36

Emma, a visually impaired student, has been receiving individualized support for her communication skills. Her teacher wants to assess her progress and make necessary adjustments. What assessment strategy would you recommend?

A. Administering a general cognitive assessment
B. Conducting a speech and language assessment
C. Consulting with Emma's parents for their observations
D. Implementing ongoing assessment through regular observations and data collection

Answer:

QUESTION 37

What factor is most likely to influence the development of orientation and mobility skills in visually impaired students?

A. Prior experience with technology
B. The level of family support and involvement
C. Physical fitness and agility
D. Exposure to bright light environments

Answer:

QUESTION 38

In order to provide effective learning experiences for visually impaired students to achieve orientation and mobility goals, which strategy should be prioritized?

- A. Minimizing exposure to real-world environments to reduce risks
- B. Focusing solely on indoor orientation training
- C. Encouraging independent problem-solving and decision-making
- D. Relying on audio-based navigation systems exclusively

Answer:

QUESTION 39

In the context of orientation and mobility development for visually impaired students, what might be a potential challenge when they rely heavily on technology for navigation?

- A. Improved spatial awareness
- B. Reduced problem-solving skills
- C. Enhanced confidence in outdoor environments
- D. Decreased reliance on auditory cues

Answer:

QUESTION 40

What is a key benefit of incorporating real-world environments into orientation and mobility training for visually impaired students?

- A. Increased reliance on technology
- B. Enhanced familiarity with indoor settings
- C. Improved ability to generalize skills
- D. Reduced exposure to sensory stimuli

Answer:

QUESTION 41

Which factor may influence a visually impaired student's motivation to develop orientation and mobility skills?

- A. Access to digital devices
- B. Teacher's expertise in orientation and mobility
- C. Desire for independence and socialization
- D. Frequent use of tactile learning materials

Answer:

QUESTION 42

What is a critical aspect of designing effective learning experiences for orientation and mobility in visually impaired students?

- A. Focusing solely on indoor navigation skills
- B. Minimizing exposure to outdoor environments
- C. Tailoring instruction to individual student needs and goals
- D. Relying solely on auditory navigation devices

Answer:

QUESTION 43

In assessing a visually impaired student's readiness for orientation and mobility training, what should be considered a primary factor?

- A. Availability of tactile learning materials
- B. Age and developmental stage of the student
- C. Access to indoor navigation apps
- D. Teacher's level of expertise

Answer:

QUESTION 44

Alex, a 14-year-old visually impaired student, has recently expressed a strong desire to participate in extracurricular sports activities like goalball, a sport designed for individuals with visual impairments. However, he has limited experience with sports. As a special education teacher, what approach should you take to support Alex's orientation and mobility skills development in the context of sports?

- A. Encourage Alex to participate but only in indoor sports to minimize risks.
- B. Recommend that Alex avoid sports as they may pose safety concerns.
- C. Provide orientation and mobility training tailored to his sports interests.
- D. Discourage sports participation and focus solely on indoor navigation.

Answer:

QUESTION 45

Emily, a visually impaired student in elementary school, often faces challenges when navigating her school's busy hallways and finding her way to different classrooms. She frequently relies on her classmates for assistance. How can you, as a special education teacher, help Emily improve her orientation and mobility skills within the school environment?

- A. Assign a classmate as a permanent guide to assist Emily.
- B. Avoid scheduling classes in different locations to minimize navigation challenges.
- C. Implement a structured orientation and mobility program.
- D. Discourage Emily from trying to navigate independently to avoid accidents.

Answer:

QUESTION 46

Jacob, a visually impaired high school student, has a strong interest in pursuing a career in music. He wants to attend a music conservatory but is concerned about navigating a new and potentially unfamiliar city on his own. What approach should you take to prepare Jacob for this transition and support his orientation and mobility needs?

- A. Discourage Jacob from pursuing a career in music due to the challenges of city navigation.
- B. Provide Jacob with a personal GPS device to rely on for navigation.
- C. Offer orientation and mobility training focused on urban navigation skills.
- D. Recommend that Jacob seek a career closer to home to avoid city navigation.

Answer:

QUESTION 47

When planning the curriculum for a visually impaired student in reading/language arts, what is a critical consideration?

A. Following the same curriculum as sighted peers to ensure consistency
B. Adapting materials and methods to accommodate the student's needs
C. Prioritizing visual content to enhance the student's understanding
D. Limiting exposure to literary genres to avoid overwhelming the student

Answer:

QUESTION 48

In teaching mathematics to a visually impaired student, what is a key strategy to promote concept development?

A. Relying solely on auditory explanations
B. Using tactile materials and hands-on activities
C. Avoiding the use of technology and digital tools
D. Providing a standardized math curriculum

Answer:

QUESTION 49

What is a potential challenge when developing a curriculum scope and sequence for a visually impaired student in science?

A. Lack of accessible science textbooks and resources
B. Overemphasizing visual content in science materials
C. Aligning the curriculum too closely with sighted peers
D. Relying solely on audio-based science instruction

Answer:

QUESTION 50

What is a key benefit of involving visually impaired students in hands-on, experiential learning activities when teaching academic skills?

A. Reducing the need for specialized materials and adaptations
B. Enhancing their problem-solving and critical thinking abilities
C. Avoiding the use of technology in the learning process
D. Minimizing the need for teacher guidance and support

Answer:

QUESTION 51

When developing the curriculum scope and sequence for a visually impaired student in social studies, what should be a primary focus?

A. Minimizing exposure to historical content to avoid information overload
B. Aligning the curriculum closely with the interests of the student
C. Omitting geography-related topics due to potential complexity
D. Adapting materials to ensure accessibility and comprehension

Answer:

QUESTION 52

What is a key strategy for promoting study skills in visually impaired students?

    A. Minimizing the use of study aids and tools
    B. Providing pre-written notes for all assignments
    C. Encouraging students to develop and use study routines
    D. Relying solely on auditory instructions for studying

Answer:

QUESTION 53

In developing the curriculum scope and sequence for a visually impaired student in reading/language arts, what should be considered a critical factor?

    A. Emphasizing visual content to enhance comprehension
    B. Focusing solely on literary genres the student is familiar with
    C. Adapting materials to address individual reading levels and interests
    D. Excluding poetry and creative writing due to potential challenges

Answer:

QUESTION 62

John, a visually impaired student, aspires to become a musician. He is passionate about playing the guitar but faces challenges due to his visual impairment. What adaptive technology or resource could best support John's pursuit of a musical career?

    A. A screen reader for musical notation
    B. Braille music notation materials
    C. A tactile metronome
    D. Extra music theory classes

Answer:

QUESTION 63

What is a primary goal when adapting instructional strategies for a visually impaired student?

    A. Maintaining consistency with traditional teaching methods
    B. Prioritizing the use of solely auditory instruction
    C. Ensuring that the student's learning preferences are met
    D. Minimizing the need for specialized materials or technologies

Answer:

QUESTION 64

What is a primary ethical consideration when working with visually impaired students in special education?

    A. Meeting the minimum legal requirements for accommodations
    B. Ensuring that all students have identical educational experiences
    C. Respecting the individual needs and preferences of each student
    D. Strictly adhering to standardized assessment practices

Answer:

QUESTION 65

You are a special education teacher for a visually impaired student. The student's parents have requested a specific assistive technology device that is not in the school's budget. What is your ethical responsibility in this situation?

A. Inform the parents that the school cannot accommodate their request.
B. Advocate for the student's needs and explore funding options or alternatives.
C. Suggest that the parents purchase the device themselves.
D. Provide the student with alternative, less expensive technology.

Answer:

QUESTION 66

What is a significant legal requirement for special education teachers working with visually impaired students?

A. Maintaining uniform teaching methods for all students
B. Providing extra support only when requested by parents
C. Ensuring that students receive a free and appropriate public education (FAPE)
D. Excluding students from standardized assessments

Answer:

QUESTION 67

When it comes to confidentiality and student records, what is a critical legal obligation for special education teachers?

A. Sharing student records with any school staff upon request
B. Disclosing student information to outside agencies without consent
C. Maintaining the privacy and confidentiality of student records
D. Keeping student records for only one academic year

Answer:

QUESTION 68

You are a teacher of students with visual impairments, and a parent has expressed concerns about their child's progress. What should be your first step in addressing these concerns ethically and professionally?

A. Reassure the parent that their concerns are unwarranted
B. Schedule a meeting with the parent to discuss their concerns and gather information
C. Ignore the concerns and focus on classroom activities
D. Request an evaluation of the student without parental involvement

Answer:

QUESTION 69

What is a key responsibility of teachers of students with visual impairments regarding assessment accommodations?

A. Providing the same accommodations for all students regardless of need
B. Advocating for the removal of all accommodations to ensure fairness
C. Determining accommodations based on individual student needs and assessments
D. Offering accommodations only when requested by parents

Answer:

QUESTION 70

You are a special education teacher for a visually impaired student. The student's Individualized Education Program (IEP) team has recommended specific accommodations and services, but the school administration is hesitant to implement them due to budget constraints. What should you do in this situation?

    A. Accept the school administration's decision and inform the IEP team.
    B. Advocate for the student's IEP recommendations and seek appropriate funding.
    C. Inform the parents that the recommended accommodations cannot be provided.
    D. Recommend that the student transfer to a different school with more resources.

Answer:

QUESTION 71

Which of the following domains of development is most directly impacted by a visual impairment in students?

    A. Cognitive development
    B. Social development
    C. Physical development
    D. Emotional development

Answer:

QUESTION 72

For visually impaired students, which domain of development might be particularly challenged due to a lack of visual cues and interactions?

    A. Social development
    B. Physical development
    C. Emotional development
    D. Language development

Answer:

QUESTION 73

What instructional strategy can be particularly effective in promoting the overall development of visually impaired students across multiple domains?

    A. Braille instruction
    B. Visual aids and charts
    C. Large-print textbooks
    D. Color-coded materials

Answer:

QUESTION 74

Which approach is most likely to facilitate the physical development of visually impaired students by enhancing their mobility and spatial awareness?

A. Encouraging the use of assistive technology
B. Providing frequent opportunities for physical activity
C. Relying solely on verbal instructions
D. Minimizing physical activities to prevent accidents

Answer:

QUESTION 75

What is the primary cause of congenital blindness in visually impaired students?

A. Traumatic injury
B. Genetic factors
C. Age-related degeneration
D. Environmental toxins

Answer:

QUESTION 76

Which visual impairment characteristic may impact a student's ability to perceive and interpret visual information such as reading materials and instructional aids?

A. Visual acuity
B. Visual field
C. Ocular motility
D. Color perception

Answer:

QUESTION 77

What is the term for a visual impairment where the field of vision is restricted, making it challenging for students to see objects to the side or in their peripheral vision?

A. Scotoma
B. Nystagmus
C. Hemianopia
D. Strabismus

Answer:

QUESTION 78

In the context of visual impairments, what is the term for an involuntary, rapid, and repetitive movement of the eyes that may affect a student's ability to focus on visual tasks?

A. Scotoma
B. Nystagmus
C. Hemianopia
D. Strabismus

Answer:

QUESTION 79

Which of the following visual impairments primarily affects the alignment of the eyes, potentially causing double vision and challenges with depth perception?

A. Scotoma
B. Nystagmus
C. Hemianopia
D. Strabismus

Answer:

QUESTION 80

Which factor is most likely to cause progressive visual impairment in students, often leading to a gradual loss of central vision?

A. Color blindness
B. Retinal degeneration
C. Amblyopia
D. Corneal scarring

Answer:

QUESTION 81

What is the term for a visual impairment where individuals have difficulty distinguishing between certain colors, which can impact their ability to access color-coded information?

A. Scotoma
B. Nystagmus
C. Hemianopia
D. Color blindness

Answer:

QUESTION 82

You have a visually impaired student in your class who is struggling with reading comprehension. Despite receiving support, their progress is slow. What is the most likely cognitive need that you should address in this case?

    A. Memory and recall
    B. Auditory processing
    C. Executive functioning
    D. Visual-spatial skills

Answer:

QUESTION 83

What cognitive skill is particularly important for visually impaired students when it comes to understanding and using language effectively?

    A. Metacognition
    B. Visual memory
    C. Logical reasoning
    D. Spatial awareness

Answer:

QUESTION 84

A visually impaired student in your class frequently struggles with initiating and maintaining conversations with peers. What aspect of language development should you focus on to support their social communication skills?

    A. Vocabulary expansion
    B. Pragmatic language skills
    C. Reading comprehension
    D. Articulation and pronunciation

Answer:

QUESTION 85

Sophia, a high school student with visual impairment, has been using a refreshable braille display for several years. She has expressed concerns about its functionality and compatibility with new technologies. What should you do? What is the most appropriate step to address Sophia's concerns about her refreshable braille display?

    A. Ignore her concerns, as the technology has been working for years.
    B. Replace the device with a new one to avoid potential issues.
    C. Collaborate with specialists to assess and upgrade the device as needed.
    D. Discourage her from using assistive technology and rely on traditional materials.

Answer:

QUESTION 86

In promoting independent living skills for a visually impaired student, what should be a key focus?

- A. Relying on others for all daily tasks
- B. Encouraging self-reliance and autonomy
- C. Avoiding any recreational activities
- D. Discouraging career aspirations

Answer:

QUESTION 87

In a case study scenario, a visually impaired student expresses interest in playing a musical instrument. How can this interest be supported effectively?

- A. Discourage the interest as it may be challenging.
- B. Provide opportunities for music lessons and adapt materials.
- C. Ignore the interest as it is unrelated to academic goals.
- D. Exclude the student from music-related activities.

Answer:

QUESTION 88

What is a crucial aspect of enhancing transition readiness for visually impaired students?

- A. Avoiding discussions about post-school goals
- B. Relying solely on academic preparation
- C. Providing vocational and career exploration experiences
- D. Disregarding students' interests and preferences

Answer:

QUESTION 89

In a case study scenario, a visually impaired student expresses a strong interest in pursuing a career in computer programming. How can this interest be supported effectively?

- A. Discourage the interest due to potential challenges.
- B. Provide access to computer programming courses and assistive technology.
- C. Ignore the interest and focus on unrelated skills.
- D. Exclude the student from technology-related activities.

Answer:

QUESTION 90

What role does self-advocacy play in enhancing transition readiness for visually impaired students?

- A. It has no relevance to transition readiness.
- B. It empowers students to communicate their needs and preferences.
- C. It solely relies on teacher advocacy.
- D. It discourages students from expressing their goals.

Answer:

QUESTION 91

In preparing visually impaired students for post-school life, what should special education teachers prioritize?

- A. Focusing solely on academic skills
- B. Ignoring vocational and career exploration
- C. Providing opportunities for skill development and practical experiences
- D. Avoiding discussions about post-school goals

Answer:

QUESTION 92

What is a key consideration when providing learning experiences to enhance transition readiness for visually impaired students?

- A. Relying solely on academic instruction
- B. Excluding students from vocational opportunities
- C. Tailoring experiences to individual interests and goals
- D. Avoiding discussions about post-school life

Answer:

QUESTION93:

Alex is a high school student with a visual impairment who wants to learn how to cook independently. However, the school lacks accessible cooking facilities. How can you support Alex in acquiring this important independent living skill? What is the most appropriate step to support Alex's goal of learning to cook independently?

- A. Discourage him from pursuing this goal due to accessibility issues.
- B. Provide resources for accessible cooking lessons outside of school.
- C. Ignore his interest in cooking as it may be challenging.
- D. Exclude him from independent living skill development.

Answer:

QUESTION 94

Sarah, a visually impaired student, expresses a strong interest in pursuing a career in graphic design. She is looking for guidance on how to explore this field effectively. What should you do to support her career aspirations? What is the most appropriate step to support Sarah's interest in a career in graphic design?

- A. Discourage her interest due to potential challenges in the field.
- B. Provide information and resources on graphic design programs and internships.
- C. Ignore her career aspirations and focus on academic subjects.
- D. Exclude her from discussions about vocational goals.

Answer:

QUESTION 95

David, a visually impaired student, is nearing graduation, and he wants to attend a university to study computer science. He's concerned about the accessibility of the university's online resources. How can you empower him to address this concern effectively? What is the most appropriate step to empower David to address concerns about the accessibility of university resources?

    A. Discourage him from pursuing a university education due to potential challenges.
    B. Teach him about self-advocacy and how to request accessible materials.
    C. Ignore his concerns about accessibility as they may be unwarranted.
    D. Exclude him from discussions about his educational goals.

Answer:

QUESTION 96

When working with agencies and services for visually impaired students, what should be a key consideration?

    A. Relying solely on school-based resources
    B. Ignoring the student's individual needs
    C. Collaborating with relevant agencies and professionals
    D. Avoiding contact with external services

Answer:

QUESTION 97

In a case study scenario, a visually impaired student requires orientation and mobility training to navigate their community independently. What is the most appropriate step to meet this need?

    A. Exclude the student from community participation.
    B. Provide written instructions for navigating the community.
    C. Collaborate with orientation and mobility specialists to develop a training plan.
    D. Discourage the student from venturing into the community.

Answer:

QUESTION 98

What is the importance of establishing positive relationships with community institutions to facilitate successful transitioning for visually impaired students?

    A. It is unnecessary, as schools can handle all aspects of transitioning.
    B. It helps ensure that community resources are leveraged for students' benefit.
    C. It focuses solely on academic preparation.
    D. It excludes the community from the transition process.

Answer:

QUESTION 99

In a case study scenario, a visually impaired student is interested in pursuing vocational training in a local trade school. How can you facilitate this transition effectively?

    A. Discourage the student from pursuing vocational training.
    B. Ignore the student's vocational interests.
    C. Establish contacts with the trade school and explore enrollment options.
    D. Exclude the student from discussions about vocational training.

Answer:

QUESTION 100

What is the significance of involving community institutions and resources in the transition planning for visually impaired students?

    A. It adds unnecessary complexity to the transition process.
    B. It ensures that transition planning remains solely within the school's control.
    C. It enhances students' access to opportunities and support.
    D. It discourages students from pursuing post-school goals.

Answer:

QUESTION 101

In transitioning students with visual impairments, what should be a primary focus when establishing relationships with community institutions?

    A. Relying solely on academic institutions for support
    B. Excluding students from the transition planning process
    C. Leveraging community resources to meet individualized needs
    D. Avoiding collaboration with community institutions

Answer:

QUESTION 102

What role does ongoing communication and collaboration with community institutions play in the successful transition of visually impaired students?

    A. It adds unnecessary complexity to the transition process.
    B. It isolates students from community support.
    C. It ensures that students have access to needed services and opportunities.
    D. It discourages students from pursuing post-school goals.

Answer:

QUESTION 103

Lisa, a visually impaired high school student, requires specialized technology and software to access digital materials. The school lacks the necessary resources. How can you ensure that Lisa receives the required technology? What is the most appropriate step to ensure that Lisa receives the necessary technology to access digital materials effectively?

A. Discourage the use of technology due to resource limitations.
B. Explore partnerships with organizations that provide assistive technology.
C. Ignore Lisa's needs for digital access.
D. Exclude Lisa from accessing digital materials.

Answer:

QUESTION 104

David, a visually impaired student, is interested in participating in a local sports league. The league has limited experience with accommodating visually impaired participants. What can be done to facilitate David's participation? What is the most appropriate step to facilitate David's participation in the local sports league that has limited experience with accommodating visually impaired participants?

A. Discourage David from pursuing sports due to potential challenges.
B. Provide a list of alternative recreational activities.
C. Establish communication with the league and explore accommodations.
D. Exclude David from participating in the league.

Answer:

QUESTION 105

What is a critical factor to consider when adapting instructional methods for teaching visually impaired students with additional disabilities?

A. Emphasizing advanced technology solutions
B. Incorporating multisensory and individualized approaches
C. Reducing the use of tactile learning materials
D. Focusing primarily on auditory instruction

Answer:

QUESTION 106

You are a special education teacher working with a visually impaired student named Emma. Emma has recently started to lose her vision due to a degenerative condition. She is struggling to adapt to her changing educational needs. How should you approach the evaluation and adaptation of instructional methods for Emma?

A. Transition Emma to a specialized school for the blind immediately.
B. Continue with her current instructional methods, as changing them may be overwhelming.
C. Conduct an assessment of Emma's current abilities and adapt instruction accordingly.
D. Recommend Emma rely solely on audio-based learning resources.

Answer:

QUESTION 107

You have a visually impaired student, Michael, who is proficient in using a white cane for mobility but has expressed interest in learning to use a guide dog. His parents are concerned about the transition. How should you handle this situation?

    A. Encourage Michael to continue with the white cane for consistency.
    B. Immediately arrange for guide dog training, as it aligns with Michael's interest.
    C. Assess Michael's goals and readiness for guide dog training and provide appropriate guidance.
    D. Ignore Michael's request, as it may be a passing interest.

Answer:

QUESTION 108

You have a visually impaired student, Ethan, who is struggling with reading and writing due to his visual impairment. You are considering introducing a screen reader as an assistive technology tool. How should you approach this decision?

    A. Purchase the screen reader software and implement it immediately.
    B. Consult with Ethan's parents and follow their guidance on assistive technology.
    C. Assess Ethan's specific needs and abilities to determine if a screen reader is suitable.
    D. Continue with traditional methods, as screen readers may be challenging for Ethan.

Answer:

QUESTION 109

You are a special education teacher working with a visually impaired student, Emily. Emily's classroom teacher is struggling to provide appropriate materials for her. What should be your initial step in addressing this situation?

    A. Provide Emily's classroom teacher with a list of materials to use.
    B. Request a meeting with Emily's parents to discuss the issue.
    C. Collaborate with Emily's classroom teacher to assess Emily's needs.
    D. Contact the school principal to intervene in the situation.

Answer:

QUESTION 110

What is a key consideration when providing training to teachers individually to support visually impaired students in the mainstream classroom?

    A. Focusing solely on the use of assistive technology
    B. Tailoring the training to the individual teacher's needs
    C. Providing generic training that applies to all teachers
    D. Conducting the training during regular classroom hours

Answer:

QUESTION 111

You are an orientation and mobility specialist working with a visually impaired student, Daniel. Daniel's physical education teacher is unsure how to include him in physical activities effectively. What should be your approach to addressing this issue?

    A. Provide Daniel's physical education teacher with written instructions.
    B. Request a meeting with the school's athletic department to discuss adaptations.
    C. Collaborate with Daniel's physical education teacher to develop tailored strategies.
    D. Advise Daniel to skip physical education classes to avoid complications.

Answer:

QUESTION 112

What is a critical factor when coordinating instruction with other teaching professionals to support a visually impaired student?

    A. Ensuring the student always has one-on-one support during instruction
    B. Communicating regularly and effectively with other professionals
    C. Limiting the student's exposure to different teaching styles
    D. Assigning all assessment tasks to a single teacher for consistency

Answer:

QUESTION 113

You are a special education teacher responsible for a visually impaired student, Ava, who requires braille materials for her coursework. The regular classroom teacher is unfamiliar with braille and is unsure how to integrate it into Ava's lessons. How should you approach this situation?

    A. Provide the regular classroom teacher with a braille textbook and ask them to figure it out.
    B. Request that Ava be placed in a specialized classroom for visually impaired students.
    C. Collaborate with the regular classroom teacher to develop strategies for integrating braille into lessons.
    D. Assign a one-on-one aide to Ava to handle all braille-related tasks.

Answer:

QUESTION 114

You are an orientation and mobility specialist working with a visually impaired student, Leo, who needs support in navigating the school environment independently. Leo's classroom teacher is concerned about his safety while moving around the campus. How should you address this concern?

    A. Suggest that Leo's classroom teacher provide constant supervision during transitions.
    B. Recommend Leo use a wheelchair to avoid mobility challenges.
    C. Collaborate with Leo's classroom teacher to assess his mobility skills and develop safety strategies.
    D. Advise Leo to rely solely on a white cane for mobility to build independence.

Answer:

QUESTION 115

You are a special education teacher responsible for a visually impaired student, Max, who requires assistive technology to access digital materials. Max's classroom teacher is uncertain about the available assistive technology options. How should you handle this situation?

A. Provide Max's classroom teacher with a list of all available assistive technologies.
B. Request that Max be placed in a specialized classroom for visually impaired students.
C. Collaborate with Max's classroom teacher to identify suitable assistive technology solutions.
D. Assign a student aide to Max to operate the assistive technology devices.

Answer:

QUESTION 116

You are a special education teacher responsible for a group of visually impaired students with varying needs. One student requires frequent one-on-one support, while others are more independent. How can you effectively manage your classroom to meet all students' needs?

A. Focus primarily on the one-on-one support student and provide less attention to independent students.
B. Assign a teacher's aide to support the independent students, allowing you to focus on the student who needs one-on-one assistance.
C. Collaborate with your school's administration to create an individualized plan for each student.
D. Develop a flexible classroom routine that combines group and individual instruction to accommodate all students.

Answer:

QUESTION 117

What is a key responsibility when applying special education-related regulations and guidelines for visually impaired students, particularly concerning equity and program development?

A. Providing identical resources and accommodations to all visually impaired students
B. Adhering strictly to standardized curricula without modifications
C. Ensuring that individualized plans and accommodations address each student's unique needs
D. Excluding visually impaired students from mainstream educational settings

Answer:

QUESTION 118

You are responsible for scheduling educational assessments for your visually impaired students. The assessments include Braille proficiency tests and orientation and mobility evaluations. How can you efficiently manage the assessment scheduling process?

A. Schedule all assessments at the same time to streamline the process.
B. Assign the responsibility of scheduling assessments to each student's parents.
C. Collaborate with the school's assessment coordinator to create a coordinated assessment schedule.
D. Conduct assessments on an ad-hoc basis whenever the students are available.

Answer:

QUESTION 119

What is a crucial aspect of applying special education-related regulations and guidelines, such as Section 504 of the Rehabilitation Act, to support visually impaired students in educational settings?

- A. Treating all students with visual impairments as if they have the same needs
- B. Adhering strictly to general education curriculum standards
- C. Providing accommodations and modifications to ensure equal access and opportunity
- D. Exempting visually impaired students from educational assessments

Answer:

QUESTION 120

What is the primary sensory modality through which visually impaired students typically acquire information and learn?

- A. Auditory
- B. Tactile
- C. Visual
- D. Olfactory

Answer:

QUESTION 121

When applying the concept of "scaffolding" from Vygotsky's sociocultural theory to visually impaired students, which of the following strategies would be most appropriate?

- A. Providing printed materials with enlarged text
- B. Encouraging independent exploration without assistance
- C. Offering verbal explanations and guided assistance as needed
- D. Using colorful visual aids for better engagement

Answer:

QUESTION 122

Which process of learning is particularly important for visually impaired students when they are learning to read and write using Braille?

- A. Classical conditioning
- B. Operant conditioning
- C. Social learning
- D. Sensorimotor learning

Answer:

QUESTION 123

When teaching visually impaired students, which of the following strategies aligns with the principles of Universal Design for Learning (UDL)?

A. Providing only auditory materials
B. Offering a variety of sensory and instructional options
C. Using exclusively visual aids
D. Assigning homework without modifications

Answer:

QUESTION 124

In the context of learning theories, which theory suggests that individuals learn by observing others and imitating their actions and behaviors?

A. Behaviorism
B. Constructivism
C. Social Learning Theory
D. Information Processing Theory

Answer:

QUESTION 125

Which of the following behaviors in a young student is most likely an indicator of a visual impairment?

A. Avoiding activities that involve close-up visual tasks
B. Reading books in dim lighting
C. Preferring bright colors in clothing
D. Asking to sit at the back of the classroom

Answer:

QUESTION 126

A student frequently squints or tilts their head while looking at objects or text. What might this behavior suggest?

A. Near-sightedness
B. Far-sightedness
C. Color blindness
D. Hearing impairment

Answer:

QUESTION 127

If a student frequently bumps into objects or people, what type of visual impairment might this behavior indicate?

A. Glaucoma
B. Cataracts
C. Retinitis pigmentosa
D. Nystagmus

Answer:

QUESTION 128

What is a potential indicator of a visual impairment when a student frequently holds objects very close to their face when examining them?

A. Normal vision development
B. Hyperopia (far-sightedness)
C. Depth perception issues
D. Retinal detachment

Answer:

QUESTION 129

If a student consistently displays poor hand-eye coordination and struggles to catch or throw objects accurately, what visual impairment might this behavior suggest?

A. Macular degeneration
B. Strabismus
C. Glaucoma
D. Diabetic retinopathy

Answer:

QUESTION 130

When a student frequently loses their place while reading, what visual impairment might be a contributing factor?

A. Night blindness
B. Nystagmus
C. Astigmatism
D. Visual field loss

Answer:

QUESTION 131

Which behavior in a student could indicate the presence of a visual impairment, particularly one affecting peripheral vision?

A. Frequent blinking
B. Holding objects very close to the eyes
C. Difficulty seeing in low light conditions
D. Frequently turning the head to the side

Answer:

QUESTION 132

A young student with a visual impairment often exhibits frustration and social withdrawal during group activities. What aspect of social/emotional development is most likely influenced by their visual impairment?

A. Peer relationships and social interaction
B. Emotional regulation and resilience
C. Self-esteem and self-concept
D. Communication and language development

Answer:

QUESTION 133

When considering the physical/motor development of a student with a visual impairment, what skill might they need extra support with to ensure safe mobility?

- A. Fine motor skills for drawing and writing
- B. Gross motor skills for running and jumping
- C. Balance and orientation for mobility
- D. Articulation and speech development

Answer:

QUESTION 134

Which functional life skill is particularly crucial for students with visual impairments to develop independence and self-sufficiency?

- A. Cooking and meal preparation
- B. Playing team sports
- C. Using a computer
- D. Visual arts and crafts

Answer:

QUESTION 135

A student with a visual impairment frequently expresses frustration and anxiety when asked to complete assignments. What common social/emotional need is likely unmet in this case?

- A. Need for assistive technology
- B. Need for peer support
- C. Need for occupational therapy
- D. Need for speech therapy

Answer:

QUESTION 136

In the context of career/vocational needs for students with visual impairments, what skill is essential for promoting successful employment?

- A. Proficiency in visual arts
- B. Strong athletic ability
- C. Effective communication skills
- D. Expertise in braille reading

Answer:

QUESTION 137

A case study a high school student with a visual impairment struggles with daily living tasks such as dressing independently. What type of specialist should the school consider involving to address this functional living need?

A. Physical therapist
B. Speech therapist
C. Occupational therapist
D. Vocational counselor

Answer:

QUESTION 138

For a student with a visual impairment, what is a common social/emotional challenge they may face due to their condition?

A. Overly aggressive behavior
B. Fear of social interactions
C. Aversion to physical activities
D. Excessive reliance on assistive devices

Answer:

QUESTION 139

When assessing functional vision in a young student, which of the following is a characteristic commonly evaluated during a formal assessment?

A. Color preferences and artistic skills
B. Eye color and pupil dilation
C. Visual acuity and visual field
D. Taste and smell sensitivity

Answer:

QUESTION 140

In a case study scenario, a visually impaired student frequently loses their place while reading Braille. Which type of assessment would be most appropriate to address this issue?

A. Formal visual acuity test
B. Informal functional vision assessment
C. Ongoing assessment of visual behavior
D. Speech and language assessment

Answer:

QUESTION 141

When conducting a formal assessment of functional vision, what does the term "visual acuity" refer to?

A. Ability to perceive colors accurately
B. Ability to see objects at a distance
C. Clarity and sharpness of vision
D. Peripheral vision range

Answer:

30

QUESTION 142

A visually impaired student exhibits difficulties in tracking moving objects and following instructions on a board during class. What type of assessment might help pinpoint the specific visual behavior challenges they are facing?

A. Formal assessment of visual field
B. Formal visual acuity test
C. Informal functional vision assessment
D. Annual vision screening

Answer:

QUESTION 143

In the context of ongoing assessment of visual behavior, what is the primary goal?

A. Identifying potential color blindness
B. Monitoring changes in visual abilities over time
C. Assessing visual acuity at a single point in time
D. Administering vision screenings regularly

Answer:

QUESTION 144

A visually impaired student is suspected of having deteriorating functional vision. What type of assessment should be used to determine the progression of their visual condition over several months?

A. A one-time functional vision assessment
B. An annual vision screening
C. Ongoing assessment of visual behavior
D. A color perception test

Answer:

QUESTION 145

When conducting a formal assessment of functional vision, what does the term "visual field" refer to?

A. The area a person can see when looking straight ahead
B. The ability to perceive colors accurately
C. The sharpness of vision at a specific distance
D. The range of peripheral vision

Answer:

QUESTION 146

Sarah is a 7-year-old student with a visual impairment. Her teacher notices that she often tilts her head to one side when reading and frequently loses her place. What initial step should the teacher take to address Sarah's reading difficulties?

A. Schedule a formal visual acuity test
B. Conduct an informal functional vision assessment
C. Recommend a speech and language assessment
D. Organize a group reading session with her peers

Answer:

QUESTION 147

Mark is a 16-year-old student with a visual impairment who has been experiencing increased difficulty in recognizing people's faces and obstacles in his path. What type of assessment is most appropriate to address his concerns?

A. An annual vision screening
B. A formal assessment of color blindness
C. An ongoing assessment of visual behavior
D. A speech and language assessment

Answer:

QUESTION 148

Emily, a 10-year-old student with a visual impairment, struggles with identifying objects in her environment and frequently knocks over items on her desk. What assessment approach should be considered to determine her specific visual needs?

A. Conduct a one-time vision screening
B. Schedule a formal visual acuity test
C. Initiate an ongoing assessment of visual behavior
D. Recommend a group art therapy session

Answer:

QUESTION 149

When developing an IEP for a visually impaired student, which component outlines the specific skills or areas where the student requires support and intervention?

A. Present Levels of Academic Achievement and Functional Performance (PLAAFP)
B. Annual goals and objectives
C. Special education services and supports
D. Parent and teacher collaboration plan

Answer:

QUESTION 150

In an IEP, what is the primary purpose of the annual goals and objectives section?

A. To list all possible accommodations for the student
B. To outline the student's preferences for learning
C. To specify measurable targets for the student's progress
D. To provide a summary of the student's past achievements

Answer:

QUESTION 151

Rachel is a visually impaired student who is working on improving her orientation and mobility skills. What should be included in her IEP to support her in this area?

- A. Goals related to improving reading fluency
- B. Goals for developing social skills
- C. Goals for enhancing braille proficiency
- D. Goals for orientation and mobility training

Answer:

QUESTION 152

When evaluating a visually impaired student's progress with respect to IEP goals and objectives, what is a critical step?

- A. Comparing the student's progress to their peers
- B. Conducting a vision assessment
- C. Reviewing the student's medical history
- D. Collecting data and evidence of the student's performance

Answer:

QUESTION 153

In an IEP, if a visually impaired student is not making sufficient progress toward their goals, what should the IEP team consider?

- A. Increasing the duration of the IEP
- B. Modifying the goals and objectives
- C. Removing special education services
- D. Holding fewer IEP meetings

Answer:

QUESTION 154

John, a visually impaired student, has made significant progress in his communication skills, surpassing his IEP goals. What should the IEP team discuss during his annual review meeting?

- A. Reducing the level of support and services
- B. Discontinuing the IEP entirely
- C. Setting new, more challenging goals
- D. Focusing on unrelated academic achievements

Answer:

QUESTION 155

In an IEP, what is the primary purpose of the Special Education Services and Supports section?

- A. To list the student's hobbies and interests
- B. To outline the school's budget for special education
- C. To specify the accommodations and services provided to the student
- D. To summarize the student's medical history

Answer:

QUESTION 156

Alex is a 9-year-old student with a visual impairment. He has been making steady progress toward his IEP goals in reading fluency. However, his recent vision assessment indicates a deterioration in his vision. What should the IEP team consider during his annual review meeting?

    A. Maintaining the same goals and objectives
    B. Discontinuing the IEP
    C. Increasing the duration of the IEP
    D. Modifying the goals to reflect his changing needs

Answer:

QUESTION 157

Sarah is a high school student with a visual impairment who has consistently exceeded her IEP goals for braille proficiency. Her teacher is considering reducing the level of support and services provided. What should the IEP team prioritize in this situation?

    A. Reducing support and services to encourage independence
    B. Discontinuing the IEP entirely
    C. Setting new, more challenging goals in braille proficiency
    D. Adding unrelated academic achievements to her IEP

Answer:

QUESTION 158

James, a visually impaired student, has an IEP that includes goals related to enhancing his orientation and mobility skills. He has made minimal progress, despite consistent support. What should the IEP team consider during his annual review?

    A. Increasing the duration of the IEP meetings
    B. Modifying the goals and objectives to better suit his needs
    C. Removing all special education services
    D. Holding fewer IEP meetings to reduce stress

Answer:

QUESTION 159

When planning sensory training activities for a visually impaired student, which of the following strategies promotes the development of tactile discrimination skills?

    A. Providing only auditory information
    B. Incorporating textured materials and objects
    C. Emphasizing visual cues and prompts
    D. Minimizing physical interactions

Answer:

QUESTION 160

Emma, a visually impaired student, has difficulty recognizing common objects by touch. Which type of sensory training activity might be most beneficial for her?

A. Listening to audio recordings
B. Engaging in braille reading exercises
C. Exploring tactile shape puzzles
D. Watching educational videos

Answer:

QUESTION 161

When evaluating instructional methods and resources for sensory training, what is a crucial consideration for visually impaired students?

A. Maximizing reliance on visual cues
B. Using exclusively auditory materials
C. Providing tactile and auditory access
D. Avoiding tactile stimulation

Answer:

QUESTION 162

Michael, a high school student with a visual impairment, is interested in learning about famous artworks. What adaptive technology might be helpful for him in this context?

A. A magnification device
B. A screen reader software
C. A braille embosser
D. A digital image-to-text converter

Answer:

QUESTION 163

When selecting adaptive and assistive technologies for sensory training, what is a key consideration for ensuring effectiveness?

A. Relying solely on mainstream technologies
B. Compatibility with the student's individual needs
C. Choosing the latest and most expensive devices
D. Minimizing the use of technology

Answer:

QUESTION 164

Julia, a visually impaired student, struggles with auditory processing and comprehension. Which assistive technology might be most helpful for her during sensory training?

    A. A braille embosser
    B. A screen reader software
    C. A hearing aid with noise cancellation
    D. A refreshable braille display

Answer:

QUESTION 165

When planning sensory training activities for visually impaired students, what is a primary goal of using adaptive and assistive technologies?

    A. Reducing sensory stimulation to avoid overwhelm
    B. Providing alternative sensory experiences
    C. Eliminating the need for tactile exploration
    D. Minimizing student engagement in the learning process

Answer:

QUESTION 166

Jordan, a 12-year-old visually impaired student, is struggling with developing tactile discrimination skills. During a sensory training session, he expresses frustration and reluctance to touch various textures. How should the teacher address this situation?

    A. Encourage Jordan to skip the tactile activities and focus on auditory training.
    B. Reduce the frequency of sensory training sessions to minimize frustration.
    C. Provide a safe and supportive environment, gradually introducing textures.
    D. Advise Jordan to use visual cues to compensate for tactile difficulties.

Answer:

QUESTION 167

Maria, a visually impaired student, is interested in exploring science concepts that involve visual diagrams. Which adaptive technology might be most beneficial for her to access visual content during science lessons?

    A. A braille embosser
    B. A digital screen reader
    C. A refreshable braille display
    D. A 3D tactile modeling kit

Answer:

QUESTION 168

David, a high school student with a visual impairment, has been working on improving his mobility skills, particularly navigating stairs. During sensory training, he expresses anxiety and reluctance to practice stair navigation. How should the teacher address David's concerns?

    A. Discourage David from practicing stair navigation due to safety concerns.
    B. Encourage David to rely solely on tactile cues during stair navigation.
    C. Provide a supportive and controlled environment for stair practice.
    D. Suggest David focus on auditory training instead.

Answer:

QUESTION 169

What is a key strategy for promoting social development in visually impaired students?

    A. Isolating them from their peers to minimize distractions
    B. Encouraging them to rely solely on auditory communication
    C. Facilitating opportunities for peer interactions and friendships
    D. Limiting their exposure to social situations to avoid potential challenges

Answer:

QUESTION 170

Sarah, a visually impaired student, is experiencing low self-esteem due to her visual impairment. What counseling approach might be most effective in helping her develop a positive self-concept?

    A. Focusing solely on academic achievements to boost self-esteem
    B. Using a strengths-based approach that highlights her abilities
    C. Avoiding discussions about self-esteem to prevent discomfort
    D. Discouraging any mention of her visual impairment to avoid stigma

Answer:

QUESTION 171

What is a key element in facilitating students' self-determination, especially for those with visual impairments?

    A. Making all decisions for the students to avoid confusion
    B. Providing limited choices to simplify decision-making
    C. Encouraging students to make choices and set goals for themselves
    D. Discouraging students from expressing their preferences

Answer:

QUESTION 172

Alex, a visually impaired student, is struggling with assertiveness in social situations. What counseling skill might be helpful in building his assertiveness skills?

A. Teaching him to avoid expressing his needs and preferences
B. Role-playing assertive communication scenarios
C. Discouraging him from speaking up in social settings
D. Isolating him from social interactions to minimize stress

Answer:

QUESTION 173

What is an essential skill for special education teachers working with visually impaired students to promote their social development?

A. Avoiding discussions about emotions and social situations
B. Practicing active listening and empathy
C. Isolating students to prevent conflicts
D. Focusing exclusively on academic skills

Answer:

QUESTION 174

James, a visually impaired student, is experiencing social adjustment challenges in his new school. What consultation skill might a special education teacher use to help James adapt and thrive?

A. Avoid discussing James's social challenges to prevent discomfort
B. Collaborate with other professionals to develop a comprehensive support plan
C. Isolate James from social situations to minimize stress
D. Discourage James from seeking help from peers or adults

Answer

QUESTION 175

What is a fundamental aspect of providing emotional support to visually impaired students?

A. Avoiding discussions about their emotions to prevent discomfort
B. Isolating students from emotional situations to protect them
C. Creating a safe and supportive environment for emotional expression
D. Discouraging students from seeking emotional support from others

Answer:

QUESTION 176

Emily, a visually impaired student, is having difficulty building friendships and often feels isolated at school. How can a special education teacher best support Emily's social development?

A. Isolate Emily from social situations to minimize potential conflicts.
B. Encourage Emily to rely solely on auditory communication to connect with peers.
C. Facilitate opportunities for peer interactions and provide social skills coaching.
D. Discourage Emily from seeking emotional support from others.

Answer:

QUESTION 177

Mark, a visually impaired student, has been feeling self-conscious about his visual impairment and lacks assertiveness in social situations. What counseling approach might be most effective in helping Mark develop assertiveness?

- A. Encourage Mark to avoid discussing his visual impairment to prevent discomfort.
- B. Isolate Mark from social interactions to minimize stress.
- C. Use a strengths-based approach that highlights his abilities and encourages assertive communication.
- D. Discourage Mark from speaking up in social settings to avoid potential conflicts.

Answer:

QUESTION 178

Sarah, a visually impaired student, is transitioning to a new school. She's experiencing social adjustment challenges and often feels overwhelmed. What consultation skill might a special education teacher use to help Sarah adapt and thrive in her new environment?

- A. Isolate Sarah from social situations to protect her from potential stress.
- B. Collaborate with other professionals to develop a comprehensive support plan for Sarah.
- C. Discourage Sarah from seeking help from peers or adults.
- D. Avoid discussing Sarah's social challenges to prevent discomfort.

Answer:

QUESTION 179

What is a fundamental strategy for establishing effective communication with families of visually impaired students, including those from diverse backgrounds?

- A. Avoid discussing the child's visual impairment to prevent discomfort
- B. Use complex and technical language to convey information
- C. Foster open, respectful, and culturally sensitive communication
- D. Discourage families from actively participating in their child's education

Answer:

QUESTION 180

Maria's parents, who are from a non-English-speaking background, have limited English proficiency. What strategy can a special education teacher use to ensure effective communication with Maria's family?

- A. Avoid involving the parents in the education process to prevent language barriers
- B. Provide written information only in English to encourage language acquisition
- C. Use bilingual staff or interpreters to facilitate communication
- D. Discourage any involvement of the parents in their child's education

Answer:

QUESTION 181

When working collaboratively with families of visually impaired students, what is a key principle to promote their participation in planning and implementing their child's education?

- A. Making decisions for the families to ensure consistency
- B. Discouraging families from sharing their input and preferences
- C. Valuing families as equal partners in the educational process
- D. Avoiding any involvement of families to minimize conflicts

Answer:

QUESTION 182

John's parents are hesitant to participate in his Individualized Education Program (IEP) meetings due to their busy work schedules. What strategy can a special education teacher use to engage John's parents more effectively?

- A. Discourage John's parents from attending IEP meetings
- B. Schedule meetings during times convenient for the teacher
- C. Offer flexible meeting times and explore alternative communication methods
- D. Avoid involving parents in the IEP process

Answer:

QUESTION 183

When collaborating with families of visually impaired students, what is a crucial consideration for promoting their active involvement in their child's education?

- A. Keeping parents uninformed about their child's progress
- B. Disregarding parents' perspectives and preferences
- C. Encouraging open and regular communication
- D. Isolating students from their families to avoid conflicts

Answer:

QUESTION 184

Lisa, a special education teacher, is working with a family who has limited access to technology and internet. How can Lisa ensure effective communication and collaboration with this family?

- A. Rely solely on digital communication methods
- B. Avoid involving the family in educational planning
- C. Use a variety of communication methods, including non-digital options
- D. Discourage the family from participating in their child's education

Answer:

QUESTION 185

What is a key component of establishing trust and positive relationships with families of visually impaired students?

- A. Avoiding interactions with families to prevent potential conflicts
- B. Providing minimal information to maintain privacy
- C. Being open, honest, and transparent in communication
- D. Excluding families from the decision-making process

Answer:

QUESTION 186

Sarah's parents are hesitant to participate in meetings and discussions about her education due to cultural differences that emphasize parental authority. How can a special education teacher effectively engage Sarah's parents in the education process?

- A. Respect their cultural beliefs and encourage open dialogue about Sarah's education.
- B. Disregard their cultural differences and proceed with decisions without them.
- C. Avoid involving Sarah's parents to prevent conflicts.
- D. Schedule meetings without considering their availability.

Answer:

QUESTION 187

Mark, a visually impaired student, has a diverse family background with varying cultural norms and values. How can a special education teacher ensure effective communication and collaboration with Mark's family?

- A. Assume a one-size-fits-all approach for communication.
- B. Ignore cultural differences to avoid potential conflicts.
- C. Adapt communication styles and approaches to be culturally sensitive.
- D. Isolate Mark's family from the educational process.

Answer:

QUESTION 188

Alex, a visually impaired student, has parents who work long hours and are often unable to attend school meetings. How can a special education teacher ensure that Alex's parents are actively involved in his education?

- A. Discourage Alex's parents from attending meetings due to their busy schedules.
- B. Schedule meetings at the convenience of the teacher.
- C. Offer flexible meeting times and explore alternative communication methods.
- D. Exclude Alex's parents from the educational planning process.

Answer:

QUESTION 189

What is a key aspect of the historical foundation of special education for visually impaired students?

- A. Exclusively focusing on segregated education settings
- B. Advocating for the exclusion of visually impaired students from education
- C. The shift towards inclusive education and mainstreaming
- D. Avoiding any formal education for visually impaired students

Answer:

QUESTION 190

Emily, a visually impaired student, is thriving in her mainstream classroom. However, she faces challenges in accessing visual content. What is a current trend that can support Emily's education?

A. Promoting the complete exclusion of visually impaired students from mainstream classrooms
B. Advancing accessible technologies and materials for visually impaired students
C. Ignoring the need for alternative formats in educational materials
D. Reducing the use of assistive technologies to minimize costs

Answer:

QUESTION 191

What is a key philosophical foundation of special education for visually impaired students?

A. Belief in the exclusion of these students from educational opportunities
B. The principle of providing equal educational opportunities and access
C. Promoting the segregation of visually impaired students
D. Avoiding any formal education for visually impaired students

Answer:

QUESTION 192

Mark, a visually impaired student, benefits from assistive technology devices. What is a current issue related to assistive technology for students like Mark?

A. The lack of advancements in assistive technology for visually impaired students
B. The high cost and limited availability of assistive technology devices
C. The complete reliance on assistive technology to replace traditional teaching methods
D. The exclusion of assistive technology in education

Answer:

QUESTION 193

What is a significant theoretical foundation that has influenced the education of visually impaired students?

A. The theory of isolating visually impaired students from mainstream education
B. The social model of disability, promoting inclusivity and accessibility
C. The theory of denying access to education for visually impaired students
D. The rejection of any theoretical foundations in special education

Answer:

QUESTION 194

Lisa, a special education teacher, is advocating for more inclusive practices in her school to support visually impaired students. What is a current trend related to inclusive education for students with visual impairments?

A. Increasing the use of segregated education settings
B. Promoting the exclusion of visually impaired students from mainstream classrooms
C. Advancing inclusive education practices and accessibility measures
D. Ignoring the needs of visually impaired students in education

Answer:

QUESTION 195

What is a current trend related to alternative delivery systems in education for visually impaired students?

- A. Decreasing the availability of alternative formats for educational materials
- B. Reducing access to remote and online learning options
- C. Advancing digital and online alternatives for educational content
- D. Promoting the use of traditional printed materials exclusively

Answer:

QUESTION 196

What is a common factor that can impede learning in visually impaired students?

- A. A quiet learning environment
- B. Accessible digital materials
- C. Lack of appropriate assistive technology
- D. Regular communication with peers

Answer:

QUESTION 197

Which of the following is a potential facilitator of learning for visually impaired students?

- A. Relying solely on printed textbooks
- B. Providing tactile graphics and braille materials
- C. Conducting lessons in a brightly lit room
- D. Minimizing verbal instructions

Answer:

QUESTION 198

What is a potential barrier to learning for visually impaired students in a mainstream classroom?

- A. Inclusion of audio descriptions in video content
- B. The availability of digital screen readers
- C. Limited awareness and understanding of visual impairment among peers and teachers
- D. Use of large print textbooks

Answer:

QUESTION 199

Which of the following strategies can help promote learning in visually impaired students?

- A. Exclusively using visual teaching aids
- B. Providing clear verbal instructions and descriptions
- C. Avoiding tactile learning experiences
- D. Limiting opportunities for independent exploration

Answer:

QUESTION 200

What factor can facilitate social interaction and learning for visually impaired students?

    A. Isolating them from peers to avoid distractions
    B. Encouraging self-reliance and independence at all times
    C. Creating opportunities for group activities and collaboration
    D. Using printed handouts as the primary mode of communication

Answer:

QUESTION 201

What is a key consideration when understanding the significance of disabilities for learning in visually impaired students?

    A. Assuming that all visually impaired students have the same needs
    B. Recognizing that disabilities do not impact learning
    C. Individualizing instruction and support based on specific needs
    D. Providing only visual materials in the classroom

Answer:

QUESTION 202

How can educators promote a growth mindset in visually impaired students?

    A. Focusing on their limitations and challenges
    B. Praising their abilities without effort
    C. Encouraging effort and perseverance in learning
    D. Avoiding discussions about their disabilities

Answer:

QUESTION 203

When assessing the learning processes of visually impaired students, what should special education teachers consider?

    A. Ignoring the impact of disabilities on learning
    B. Overemphasizing the use of visual materials
    C. Utilizing multiple forms of assessment
    D. Providing one-size-fits-all accommodations

Answer:

QUESTION 204

What role does self-advocacy play in the learning process of visually impaired students?

    A. It has no relevance to their learning.
    B. It empowers students to communicate their needs and preferences.
    C. It relies solely on teacher advocacy.
    D. It discourages independence.

Answer:

QUESTION 205

How can understanding the significance of disabilities for learning benefit educators working with visually impaired students?

- A. It allows educators to ignore individual needs.
- B. It helps educators provide one-size-fits-all solutions.
- C. It enables educators to tailor instruction and support.
- D. It encourages educators to focus solely on visual materials.

Answer:

QUESTION 206

In what way can collaborative partnerships with families benefit the learning process of visually impaired students?

- A. By excluding families from the educational process
- B. By limiting communication with families
- C. By fostering a supportive and informed network
- D. By solely relying on teacher expertise

Answer:

QUESTION 207

When adapting learning materials for visually impaired students, what should educators prioritize?

- A. Exclusively using visual materials
- B. Ignoring individual preferences
- C. Incorporating accessible formats
- D. Relying on the same materials for all students

Answer:

QUESTION 208

When teaching a visually impaired student to use low vision aids, what is an essential step in the process?

- A. Discouraging their use in the classroom
- B. Avoiding hands-on practice with the aids
- C. Providing proper training and guidance
- D. Assuming they can figure it out independently

Answer:

QUESTION 209

In a case study scenario, a visually impaired student has difficulty using their low vision aid in a busy classroom. What should the teacher do?

- A. Immediately remove the low vision aid to avoid distraction
- B. Provide additional support and strategies to use the aid effectively
- C. Ignore the issue and continue with the lesson
- D. Isolate the student from the classroom environment

Answer:

QUESTION 210

What is a key consideration when determining the appropriateness of using low vision aids for a visually impaired student?

A. The cost of the aids
B. The severity of the impairment
C. The availability of the aids in the market
D. The student's personal preference

Answer:

QUESTION 211

When is it appropriate to use low vision aids for a visually impaired student in an educational setting?

A. Only when no other accommodations are available
B. In all situations, regardless of the student's needs
C. When they enhance the student's access to information and learning
D. Only during specific subjects like art or music

Answer:

QUESTION 212

In a case study scenario, a visually impaired student is struggling with using low vision aids during art class. What should the teacher consider?

A. Eliminating art class from the curriculum
B. Providing alternative ways for the student to engage in art
C. Forcing the student to use the aids without adjustments
D. Ignoring the student's struggles

Answer:

QUESTION 213

Which of the following is a recommended procedure for introducing low vision aids to a visually impaired student?

A. Handing over the aids without explanation
B. Encouraging the student to figure it out independently
C. Providing clear instruction and guided practice
D. Avoiding any discussion about the aids

Answer:

QUESTION 214

What role can collaboration with vision specialists play in determining the appropriateness of low vision aids for a student?

A. It has no impact on the decision-making process.
B. It can provide valuable insights into the student's needs and options.
C. Collaboration is solely the responsibility of the student.
D. It can delay the use of low vision aids unnecessarily.

Answer:

QUESTION 215

When interpreting assessment results for a visually impaired student, what should special education teachers consider as a priority?

A. Relying solely on standardized test scores
B. Collaborating with medical professionals
C. Evaluating the impact of the visual impairment on learning
D. Ignoring the assessment results

Answer:

QUESTION 216

In a case study scenario, a visually impaired student receives a clinical report that mentions visual acuity measurements. What should the teacher do with this information?

A. Disregard the measurements as irrelevant to the student's education
B. Use the measurements to develop appropriate instructional strategies
C. Share the measurements with the student's peers for awareness
D. Immediately modify the curriculum based on the measurements

Answer:

QUESTION 217

What is the significance of considering assessment results when planning instruction for visually impaired students?

A. To label the student's disability
B. To create one-size-fits-all teaching approaches
C. To inform individualized and targeted instruction
D. To disregard the student's needs

Answer:

QUESTION 218

When interpreting assessment results for a visually impaired student, what should be a priority in fostering a collaborative approach?

A. Avoiding collaboration with other professionals
B. Ignoring input from the student and their family
C. Seeking input from medical specialists and educators
D. Relying solely on the teacher's expertise

Answer:

QUESTION 219

In a case study scenario, a visually impaired student's assessment indicates difficulty with visual-motor integration. What should the teacher consider when planning instruction?

A. Exclusively focusing on visual-motor activities
B. Disregarding the assessment results as unreliable
C. Incorporating strategies to support visual-motor skills development
D. Relying solely on auditory instruction

Answer:

QUESTION 220

What should special education teachers avoid when interpreting assessment results for visually impaired students?

    A. Seeking input from the student and their family
    B. Making assumptions about the student's abilities based solely on assessment scores
    C. Collaborating with other professionals
    D. Ignoring the impact of the visual impairment

Answer:

QUESTION 221

How can the interpretation of assessment results benefit visually impaired students?

    A. By categorizing them based on their disability
    B. By providing a one-size-fits-all curriculum
    C. By informing individualized support and interventions
    D. By ignoring their unique needs

Answer:

QUESTION 222

When modifying the learning environment for visually impaired students, what is a key consideration?

    A. Maximizing the use of visual materials
    B. Providing a one-size-fits-all approach
    C. Individualizing accommodations based on student needs
    D. Excluding them from group activities

Answer:

QUESTION 223

In a case study scenario, a visually impaired student is struggling with accessing printed materials in a mainstream classroom. What should the teacher consider?

    A. Continuing with printed materials to promote independence
    B. Providing accessible alternatives like braille or digital texts
    C. Ignoring the student's difficulties
    D. Isolating the student from classroom activities

Answer:

QUESTION 224

What is an essential aspect of physical and medical management for students with physical and health impairments?

    A. Relying solely on general education teachers for management
    B. Collaborating with healthcare professionals for specialized care
    C. Ignoring the need for specialized equipment
    D. Avoiding discussions about the student's health

Answer:

QUESTION 225

In the context of physical management, what should be considered when designing an inclusive classroom environment for a student with mobility challenges?

A. Providing only stairs for accessibility
B. Ensuring the classroom is located on the upper floors of a building
C. Incorporating ramps and accessible seating options
D. Ignoring the need for physical accommodations

Answer:

QUESTION 226

What is a key goal of individual and group management strategies for visually impaired students in an inclusive classroom?

A. Isolating visually impaired students from their peers
B. Maintaining strict control over behavior
C. Maximizing time spent in learning and promoting positive behavior
D. Ignoring the need for behavior management

Answer:

QUESTION 227

In a case study scenario, a visually impaired student frequently disrupts class with outbursts. What should the teacher consider when developing management strategies?

A. Isolating the student from the classroom to avoid disruptions
B. Collaborating with specialists to address the underlying causes
C. Ignoring the disruptive behavior
D. Assigning additional homework as punishment

Answer:

QUESTION 228

What is the importance of using positive reinforcement in individual and group management strategies for visually impaired students?

A. To solely focus on punishment as a behavior modification tool
B. To establish a positive and supportive classroom environment
C. To avoid addressing behavioral issues altogether
D. To rely on negative reinforcement as the primary strategy

Answer:

QUESTION 229

Sarah is a visually impaired student in your inclusive classroom. She struggles with accessing printed materials and has been feeling excluded during group activities. How can you modify the learning environment to better support Sarah? What is the most appropriate modification to support Sarah's inclusion and learning in the classroom?

    A. Continue using printed materials to encourage independence.
    B. Provide accessible alternatives like braille or digital texts.
    C. Exclude her from group activities to avoid frustration.
    D. Ignore her difficulties and focus on other students' needs.

Answer:

QUESTION 230

James is a student with a physical impairment that affects his mobility. He uses a wheelchair to navigate the school. The classroom is on the second floor, and there is no elevator. What should be done to ensure James's access to the classroom? What is the most appropriate action to ensure James can access the classroom on the second floor?

    A. Encourage James to use the stairs to promote independence.
    B. Relocate the classroom to the ground floor.
    C. Install a ramp or lift to make the classroom accessible.
    D. Assign a personal assistant to carry James up the stairs.

Answer:

QUESTION 231

In your inclusive classroom, you have a visually impaired student named Emma who frequently disrupts the class with outbursts. Her disruptive behavior is affecting the learning environment for all students. What should you do to address this situation effectively? What is the most appropriate step to address Emma's disruptive behavior and maintain a positive learning environment for all students?

    A. Isolate Emma from the classroom to avoid disruptions.
    B. Assign additional homework as a form of punishment.
    C. Collaborate with specialists to understand and address the underlying causes.
    D. Ignore Emma's disruptive behavior and focus on teaching.

Answer:

QUESTION 232

When evaluating instructional methods for a student with a visual impairment, what should be the primary consideration?

    A. Prioritizing traditional visual learning approaches
    B. Ignoring the use of adaptive technologies
    C. Tailoring methods to the individual student's needs
    D. Promoting visual learning exclusively

Answer:

QUESTION 233

In a case study scenario, a visually impaired student is struggling to access digital materials. What is a possible solution to support the student's access to technology?

    A. Provide the student with printed materials only.
    B. Offer training on screen readers or other assistive technologies.
    C. Discourage the use of technology in the classroom.
    D. Ignore the issue as technology may not be suitable.

Answer:

QUESTION 234

What is the primary goal of adapting instructional resources for students with visual impairments?

    A. Eliminating the need for instructional resources
    B. Replicating traditional visual materials exactly
    C. Ensuring equal access to educational materials
    D. Ignoring the use of adapted resources

Answer:

QUESTION 235

In the selection of adaptive and assistive technologies for a student with visual impairment, what should be a key consideration?

    A. Choosing technologies that are not user-friendly
    B. Prioritizing cost over functionality
    C. Tailoring technologies to the student's specific needs
    D. Avoiding the use of technology altogether

Answer:

QUESTION 236

In a case study scenario, a visually impaired student prefers using braille materials, but the school primarily provides printed textbooks. What should the teacher consider when selecting instructional resources?

    A. Continue using printed materials exclusively.
    B. Provide braille materials as the primary resource.
    C. Explore options to provide both printed and braille materials.
    D. Ignore the student's preference.

Answer:

QUESTION 237

What is the significance of ongoing evaluation when using adaptive and assistive technologies for students with visual impairments?

    A. Ongoing evaluation is unnecessary.
    B. It helps ensure the technologies remain current and effective.
    C. It should be done annually, regardless of changes in the student's needs.
    D. It focuses solely on the cost-effectiveness of the technologies.

Answer:

QUESTION 238

When adapting instructional methods for a visually impaired student, what is the ultimate goal?

    A. To eliminate the need for adaptations
    B. To replicate traditional visual methods exactly
    C. To maximize the student's access to instruction
    D. To rely solely on traditional teaching approaches

Answer:

QUESTION 239

You have a new student, Emily, who is visually impaired. You need to evaluate and select appropriate instructional methods and resources for her. She expresses a strong interest in science, and the standard science curriculum is primarily visual. What should you consider? What is the most appropriate step to ensure effective instruction for Emily in science?

    A. Assign her to a different class without science.
    B. Provide her with only visual materials to match the standard curriculum.
    C. Collaborate with specialists to adapt science materials into accessible formats.
    D. Discourage her interest in science and steer her towards other subjects.

Answer:

QUESTION 240

John, a visually impaired student, has been using a screen reader successfully to access digital content. However, he recently encountered challenges with specific websites that are not screen reader-friendly. What should you do? What is the most appropriate action to address John's challenges with screen reader accessibility?

    A. Remove access to digital content to avoid further issues.
    B. Continue using the screen reader without addressing the challenges.
    C. Explore alternative screen reader options.
    D. Collaborate with website developers to improve accessibility.

Answer:

QUESTION 241

Sophia, a visually impaired student, aspires to pursue a career in music production after high school. However, the school lacks resources for music production training. How can you support Sophia's career aspirations? What is the most appropriate step to support Sophia's career aspirations in music production when the school lacks resources for training?

    A. Discourage Sophia from pursuing a career in music production.
    B. Ignore Sophia's career interests and focus solely on academic subjects.
    C. Establish connections with local music production studios and explore training opportunities.
    D. Exclude Sophia from discussions about career goals.

Answer:

QUESTION 242

What is the primary focus of the history and philosophy of special education regarding students with visual impairments?

    A. The exclusion of visually impaired students from education
    B. Ensuring that visually impaired students receive the same education as their sighted peers
    C. Ignoring the historical context of education for visually impaired students
    D. Excluding philosophy from the discussion of education for visually impaired students

Answer:

QUESTION 243

In the historical context of education for visually impaired students, what significant development marked a turning point toward inclusion and accessible education?

    A. The establishment of segregated schools for visually impaired students
    B. The introduction of specialized braille instruction
    C. The integration of visually impaired students into mainstream schools
    D. The complete exclusion of visually impaired students from education

Answer:

QUESTION 244

What is one key issue in the education of visually impaired students that has gained significant attention in recent years?

    A. Ignoring individualized instruction
    B. The lack of assistive technology
    C. The importance of early intervention
    D. Excluding visually impaired students from extracurricular activities

Answer:

QUESTION 245

What is one significant trend in the education of visually impaired students that has emerged due to advancements in technology?

    A. A decline in braille literacy
    B. An increased reliance on print materials
    C. The growth of digital accessibility and e-books
    D. Excluding visually impaired students from technology use

Answer:

QUESTION 246

What is the importance of research in the field of education for visually impaired students?

    A. To exclude evidence-based practices
    B. To maintain the status quo in education
    C. To identify effective strategies and interventions
    D. To discourage the use of data and evidence

Answer:

QUESTION 247

In recent research related to education for visually impaired students, what has been a focus area to enhance their learning experiences?

A. Relying solely on traditional teaching methods
B. Promoting exclusion from mainstream classrooms
C. Exploring the use of inclusive practices and access to curriculum
D. Ignoring the significance of research in education

Answer:

QUESTION 248

What is one key challenge in conducting research related to education for visually impaired students?

A. Lack of interest from researchers
B. Limited access to research funding and resources
C. Overemphasis on exclusionary practices
D. Ignoring the role of research in education

Answer:

QUESTION 249

What is one potential challenge that visually impaired students may face when learning in a mainstream classroom environment?

A. Limited access to visual materials
B. Difficulty in understanding spoken language
C. Difficulty in understanding tactile information
D. Difficulty in participating in physical activities

Answer:

QUESTION 250

When working with a culturally diverse group of visually impaired students, what should a teacher consider?

A. The importance of inclusive teaching methods
B. Ignoring cultural differences to focus on the visual impairment
C. Providing specialized materials only for visually impaired students
D. Limiting exposure to diverse cultural experiences

Answer:

QUESTION 251

How might a teacher modify a lesson on a famous work of art for a visually impaired student?

A. Provide a tactile representation of the artwork
B. Ask the student to analyze the visual elements of the artwork
C. Play an audio recording of the art critic's analysis
D. Assign a written essay on the artwork's visual details

Answer:

QUESTION 252

In what way can a visual impairment impact a student's reading abilities?

    A. Difficulty in tracking lines of text
    B. Limited understanding of syntax and grammar
    C. Enhanced visual memory for written material
    D. Increased speed in reading comprehension

Answer:

QUESTION 253

When planning a lesson for a visually impaired student who speaks English as a second language, what should a teacher consider?

    A. Providing multi-modal instructional materials
    B. Focusing solely on language instruction
    C. Avoiding tactile materials to reduce confusion
    D. Using only visual aids for instruction

Answer:

QUESTION 254

Which part of the eye is responsible for controlling the amount of light entering the eye and thus plays a crucial role in regulating visual clarity?

    A. Retina
    B. Cornea
    C. Pupil
    D. Lens

Answer:

QUESTION 255

What is the primary function of the retina in the visual system?

    A. To control the size of the pupil
    B. To focus light onto the cornea
    C. To convert light into electrical signals
    D. To protect the eye from dust and debris

Answer:

QUESTION 256

Which condition is characterized by the gradual loss of central vision, often resulting in a "tunnel vision" effect?

    A. Glaucoma
    B. Macular degeneration
    C. Cataracts
    D. Retinitis pigmentosa

Answer:

QUESTION 257

What visual condition is characterized by clouding or opacity of the eye's natural lens, leading to blurred vision?

A. Glaucoma
B. Strabismus
C. Cataracts
D. Color blindness

Answer:

QUESTION 258

When working with a student who has low vision, what should a teacher consider when selecting classroom materials?

A. Using high-contrast materials
B. Avoiding tactile materials
C. Relying solely on auditory resources
D. Minimizing the use of lighting

Answer:

QUESTION 259

What is the primary goal of orientation and mobility training for visually impaired students?

A. To improve peripheral vision
B. To enhance color recognition
C. To develop independent travel skills
D. To increase visual acuity

Answer:

QUESTION 260

In the context of visual impairments, what does the term "Braille" refer to?

A. A form of sign language
B. A tactile writing system
C. A visual chart for tracking eye movement
D. A type of assistive technology device

Answer:

QUESTION 261

A student with low vision is struggling to read standard print. Which optical principle is most relevant in determining the appropriate low vision aid for this student?

A. Refraction
B. Magnification
C. Dispersion
D. Reflection

Answer:

QUESTION 262

What type of low vision aid is designed to enhance distance vision and is often used for activities like watching a presentation in a classroom?

- A. Telescopes
- B. Magnifiers
- C. Absorptive filters
- D. Prism glasses

Answer:

QUESTION 263

In a case study, a student with low vision struggles with glare from bright lights, which hinders their ability to read. Which type of low vision aid would be most beneficial for this student?

- A. Absorptive filters
- B. Magnifiers
- C. Prism glasses
- D. Telescopes

Answer:

QUESTION 264

A visually impaired student is having difficulty with tasks that require both hands, such as writing while referring to a textbook. Which type of low vision aid could help address this issue?

- A. Stand magnifier
- B. Handheld magnifier
- C. Video magnifier
- D. Prism glasses

Answer:

QUESTION 265

When choosing a low vision aid for a student, what is a crucial factor to consider alongside magnification?

- A. Field of view
- B. Lens color
- C. Material durability
- D. Weight of the device

Answer:

QUESTION 266

A student with low vision needs to read a book for an assignment. They prefer a portable aid. Which type of low vision aid would be most suitable for this situation?

A. Handheld magnifier
B. Stand magnifier
C. Telescopes
D. Prism glasses

Answer:

QUESTION 267

What characteristic of low vision aids is particularly important for a student who enjoys outdoor activities like birdwatching?

A. Weather resistance
B. Maximum magnification
C. Absorptive capabilities
D. Prism adjustability

Answer:

QUESTION 268

In assessing a visually impaired student's academic achievement, which type of assessment would be most appropriate for evaluating their reading comprehension skills?

A. Informal Reading Inventory (IRI)
B. Multiple-Choice Test
C. Standardized IQ Test
D. Parent naire

Answer:

QUESTION 269

A visually impaired student has recently shown improvements in their mathematics skills. What type of assessment would be most useful for monitoring their progress over time?

A. Curriculum-Based Measurement (CBM)
B. Case Study Analysis
C. Norm-Referenced Test
D. Self-Assessment

Answer:

QUESTION 270

In a case study scenario, a visually impaired student demonstrates exceptional problem-solving abilities in practical situations, but struggles with written tests. What type of assessment strategy would be most effective in capturing the student's true abilities?

A. Performance-Based Assessment
B. Multiple-Choice Test
C. Observational Checklist
D. IQ Test

Answer:

QUESTION 271

What is a crucial consideration when interpreting assessment results for a visually impaired student?

A. Differentiation between visual and non-visual factors affecting performance
B. Relying solely on standardized scores for interpretation
C. Ignoring cultural background in assessment interpretation
D. Focusing exclusively on intellectual performance

Answer:

QUESTION 272

When conducting ongoing assessments for a visually impaired student, what is a key advantage of using technology-based assessment tools?

A. Accessibility features for visually impaired students
B. Reduced need for teacher involvement in assessment
C. Elimination of performance anxiety in students
D. Standardized administration across all students

Answer:

QUESTION 273

In a case study, a visually impaired student excels in hands-on science experiments but struggles with written reports. What assessment approach would best capture their true understanding of the subject?

A. Portfolio Assessment
B. Standardized Test
C. Oral Presentation
D. True/False Test

Answer:

QUESTION 274

When communicating assessment results to parents of a visually impaired student, what is a key aspect to consider?

A. Providing specific examples of the student's strengths and areas for improvement
B. Using technical language to convey assessment terminology
C. Minimizing the importance of parental involvement in the student's education
D. Avoiding discussions about accommodations or modifications

Answer:

QUESTION 275

Sarah is a visually impaired student who has recently transferred to a new school. The special education teacher wants to assess Sarah's academic achievement levels to provide appropriate support. Which assessment method would be most effective in this situation?

A. Curriculum-Based Measurement (CBM)
B. IQ Test
C. Parent naire
D. Multiple-Choice Test

Answer:

QUESTION 276

Michael is a visually impaired student who excels in hands-on science experiments but struggles with written assessments. The teacher wants to accurately evaluate Michael's understanding of the subject. What assessment approach would be most appropriate in this situation?

A. Performance-Based Assessment
B. Standardized Test
C. True/False Test
D. Multiple-Choice Test

Answer:

QUESTION 277

Alex, a visually impaired student, has consistently shown improvements in reading fluency and comprehension over the past few months. The teacher wants to continue monitoring Alex's progress in reading. What assessment tool would be most suitable for ongoing assessment?

A. Informal Reading Inventory (IRI)
B. Standardized IQ Test
C. Self-Assessment
D. Case Study Analysis

Answer:

QUESTION 278

In a diverse classroom that includes visually impaired students, what is a crucial factor in establishing a productive learning environment?

A. Culturally responsive teaching practices
B. Relying solely on standardized assessments
C. Minimizing the use of tactile materials
D. Ignoring individual learning styles

Answer:

QUESTION 279

A visually impaired student in your class is experiencing challenges with self-esteem. What strategy would be most effective in addressing this issue?

A. Encouraging peer collaboration and support
B. Focusing exclusively on individual tasks and assignments
C. Minimizing opportunities for independent decision-making
D. Avoiding discussions about diversity and inclusion

Answer:

QUESTION 280

In a case study scenario, a visually impaired student expresses frustration with accessing classroom materials. What proactive steps can a teacher take to address this concern?

A. Provide materials in accessible formats (e.g., Braille, large print)
B. Disregard the student's concerns and maintain current materials
C. Assign a peer to transcribe materials for the student
D. Limit the use of tactile materials to reduce confusion

Answer:

QUESTION 281

What is a key factor in creating a learning environment that positively influences students' attitudes toward learning, particularly for visually impaired students?

A. Fostering a sense of belonging and inclusivity
B. Maintaining a strictly structured and inflexible classroom
C. Avoiding discussions about diversity and cultural differences
D. Relying solely on visual aids for instruction

Answer:

QUESTION 282

In a diverse classroom, how can a teacher proactively address cultural and language differences among visually impaired students?

A. Incorporate diverse perspectives and materials into the curriculum
B. Minimize opportunities for peer interaction and collaboration
C. Use standardized assessments exclusively for evaluation
D. Avoid discussing cultural differences in the classroom

Answer:

QUESTION 283

A visually impaired student is struggling with self-esteem issues related to their visual impairment. What is an effective strategy for addressing this concern?

   A. Encourage the student to engage in activities that showcase their strengths
   B. Disregard the issue, as it is unrelated to academic performance
   C. Minimize opportunities for the student to interact with peers
   D. Discourage the student from discussing their visual impairment

Answer:

QUESTION 284

In a classroom with visually impaired students, what is a crucial factor in establishing a smoothly functioning learning environment?

   A. Providing clear and consistent communication
   B. Limiting opportunities for student collaboration
   C. Ignoring individual learning styles and preferences
   D. Using exclusively visual materials for instruction

Answer:

QUESTION 285

Maria, a visually impaired student, recently joined your class. She comes from a culturally diverse background and speaks English as a second language. How can you best support Maria's transition and ensure she feels included in the learning environment?

   A. Provide materials in accessible formats and consider incorporating elements of her cultural background into lessons.
   B. Rely solely on visual aids for instruction to accommodate her visual impairment.
   C. Encourage Maria to communicate primarily with peers who share her cultural and linguistic background.
   D. Minimize opportunities for group activities to avoid potential communication barriers.

Answer:

QUESTION 286

John, a visually impaired student, has shown a keen interest in technology. He is eager to explore digital learning resources. How can you leverage John's interest in technology to enhance his learning experience?

   A. Provide access to assistive technology tools and resources that cater to John's specific needs.
   B. Discourage John from using technology as it may hinder his social interaction skills.
   C. Limit John's exposure to technology to prevent over-reliance on digital resources.
   D. Avoid discussing technology options with John as it may overwhelm him.

Answer:

QUESTION 287

Raj, a visually impaired student, has been struggling with self-esteem issues due to his visual impairment. What can you do as a teacher to address Raj's self-esteem and create a supportive learning environment?

A. Foster a classroom culture that celebrates diversity and emphasizes each student's unique strengths.
B. Avoid discussing Raj's visual impairment to prevent drawing attention to it.
C. Encourage Raj to primarily interact with peers who do not have visual impairments.
D. Provide extra academic support to compensate for Raj's self-esteem challenges.

Answer:

QUESTION 288

A newly enrolled student, Jane, has a visual impairment and is eager to learn braille. What is the initial step a teacher should take to support Jane's readiness to read in braille?

A. Conduct a braille assessment to determine her current skill level.
B. Provide Jane with advanced braille materials to challenge her.
C. Focus solely on auditory learning techniques to build her readiness.
D. Delay braille instruction until Jane expresses more interest.

Answer:

QUESTION 289

David, a visually impaired student, excels in using technology for communication. Which strategy would be most effective in meeting David's expressive and receptive language goals?

A. Providing training in keyboarding skills and accessible technology options.
B. Limiting David's access to technology to promote other forms of communication.
C. Focusing exclusively on traditional braille instruction.
D. Disregarding technology in favor of verbal communication.

Answer:

QUESTION 290

In a case study scenario, Emily, a visually impaired student, has shown a strong interest in exploring advanced math concepts using Nemeth code. How can a teacher best support Emily's learning in this area?

A. Provide instruction in Nemeth code and offer challenging math materials.
B. Discourage Emily from pursuing advanced math concepts to prevent frustration.
C. Focus solely on tactile learning methods for math instruction.
D. Avoid discussing Nemeth code to prevent overwhelming Emily.

Answer:

QUESTION 291

How can a teacher promote effective expressive language development for visually impaired students who are learning braille?

    A. Encourage students to participate in writing activities using braille.
    B. Rely solely on auditory methods for expressive language instruction.
    C. Discourage the use of braille in favor of verbal communication.
    D. Provide materials exclusively in large print.

Answer:

QUESTION 292

Sarah, a visually impaired student, prefers using a refreshable braille display for reading and writing. How can a teacher best support Sarah's learning experience?

    A. Ensure access to a refreshable braille display and provide instruction on its use.
    B. Discourage the use of technology in favor of traditional braille materials.
    C. Limit Sarah's access to braille displays to prevent over-reliance on technology.
    D. Focus exclusively on auditory learning methods.

Answer:

QUESTION 293

In a case study scenario, Tom, a visually impaired student, is struggling with braille literacy. What proactive steps can a teacher take to address this concern?

    A. Provide additional braille instruction and offer varied materials to engage Tom's interests.
    B. Discourage Tom from pursuing braille literacy to reduce potential frustration.
    C. Focus solely on auditory learning methods for Tom's instruction.
    D. Avoid discussing braille literacy to prevent overwhelming Tom.

Answer:

QUESTION 294

How can a teacher effectively address the communication needs of visually impaired students who have diverse learning styles and preferences?

    A. Provide a range of communication options, including braille, auditory methods, and technology.
    B. Focus exclusively on verbal communication to ensure consistency.
    C. Disregard individual learning styles and use a one-size-fits-all approach.
    D. Minimize the use of technology to avoid overwhelming students.

Answer:

QUESTION 295

Alex is a visually impaired student who has been struggling with braille literacy. Despite receiving instruction, he still faces challenges in reading and writing braille. What proactive steps can a teacher take to support Alex's braille literacy development?

- A. Conduct a comprehensive assessment to identify specific areas of difficulty and tailor instruction accordingly.
- B. Suggest that Alex solely rely on auditory learning methods to ease the burden of braille literacy.
- C. Discourage Alex from pursuing braille literacy to prevent further frustration.
- D. Provide only traditional braille materials without considering Alex's interests.

Answer:

QUESTION 296

Emily, a visually impaired student, has shown a keen interest in learning the Nemeth code to access advanced math materials. How can a teacher best facilitate Emily's learning experience with the Nemeth code?

- A. Provide dedicated instruction in the Nemeth code and offer a range of challenging math materials.
- B. Discourage Emily from exploring the Nemeth code due to its complexity.
- C. Focus exclusively on tactile learning methods without introducing the Nemeth code.
- D. Avoid discussing the Nemeth code to prevent overwhelming Emily.

Answer:

QUESTION 297

James, a visually impaired student, has a preference for using a refreshable braille display for reading and writing. How can a teacher best accommodate James's learning preferences and optimize his learning experience?

- A. Ensure James has consistent access to a refreshable braille display and provide guidance on its effective use.
- B. Discourage the use of technology in favor of traditional braille materials.
- C. Limit James's access to the braille display to avoid over-reliance on technology.
- D. Focus exclusively on auditory learning methods for James's instruction.

Answer:

QUESTION 298

Emma, a visually impaired student, is struggling with social interactions and building friendships. What is a proactive step a teacher can take to support Emma's social/emotional development?

- A. Provide opportunities for structured social activities with peers, incorporating inclusive games and cooperative tasks.
- B. Discourage Emma from engaging in social activities to prevent potential discomfort.
- C. Avoid discussing social interactions to prevent overwhelming Emma.
- D. Focus exclusively on individual academic tasks.

Answer:

QUESTION 299

How can a teacher effectively incorporate adaptive and assistive technologies to support the social/emotional development of visually impaired students?

A. Provide access to technologies that facilitate communication and social interactions, such as screen readers and social media platforms with accessibility features.
B. Discourage the use of technology to encourage face-to-face interactions exclusively.
C. Minimize the use of adaptive and assistive technologies to avoid overwhelming students.
D. Use technology solely for academic purposes, excluding social/emotional development.

Answer:

QUESTION 300

In a case study scenario, Jake, a visually impaired student, is experiencing difficulty expressing his emotions and managing frustration. What approach can a teacher take to address Jake's social/emotional development?

A. Implement strategies for emotional regulation and provide opportunities for Jake to express his feelings through art or journaling.
B. Discourage Jake from expressing emotions to maintain a calm classroom environment.
C. Minimize discussions about emotions to prevent overwhelming Jake.
D. Focus exclusively on academic tasks without addressing social/emotional development.

Answer:

QUESTION 301

What is a crucial consideration when evaluating and selecting instructional methods for promoting the social/emotional development of visually impaired students?

A. Recognizing individual strengths, challenges, and preferences of each student.
B. Implementing a one-size-fits-all approach for efficiency.
C. Disregarding the emotional well-being of students to prioritize academic achievement.
D. Minimizing opportunities for peer interactions to avoid potential conflicts.

Answer:

QUESTION 302

How can a teacher address potential barriers to social/emotional development for visually impaired students in a mainstream classroom?

A. Foster a supportive and inclusive classroom environment by promoting understanding, empathy, and open communication among all students.
B. Isolate visually impaired students from their peers to prevent potential conflicts.
C. Focus solely on academic instruction without considering social/emotional development.
D. Minimize opportunities for group activities to avoid potential challenges.

Answer:

QUESTION 303

In a case study scenario, Lily, a visually impaired student, expresses interest in joining extracurricular activities but is hesitant due to her visual impairment. How can a teacher support Lily's social/emotional development in this situation?

    A. Provide encouragement, facilitate discussions about Lily's interests, and explore accommodations or modifications to ensure her participation in extracurricular activities.

    B. Discourage Lily from joining extracurricular activities to prevent potential challenges.

    C. Minimize discussions about extracurricular activities to prevent overwhelming Lily.

    D. Focus exclusively on academic tasks without addressing extracurricular interests.

Answer:

QUESTION 304

What is an important aspect of using adaptive and assistive technologies to support social/emotional development in visually impaired students?

    A. Ensuring that technologies are selected based on individual needs and preferences, and providing appropriate training and support for their use.

    B. Using technology solely for academic purposes without considering social/emotional development.

    C. Minimizing the use of adaptive and assistive technologies to avoid dependence on technology.

    D. Discouraging the use of technology to promote face-to-face interactions exclusively.

Answer:

QUESTION 305

Oliver, a visually impaired student, has recently started attending a mainstream school. He is struggling to form connections with his classmates and often feels isolated. How can a teacher best support Oliver's social/emotional development in this situation?

    A. Facilitate small group activities that encourage teamwork and collaboration among students, ensuring Oliver's active participation.

    B. Discourage Oliver from seeking social interactions to avoid potential discomfort.

    C. Minimize opportunities for group activities to prevent potential conflicts.

    D. Focus exclusively on academic tasks without addressing Oliver's social/emotional needs.

Answer:

QUESTION 306

Sophie, a visually impaired student, is showing signs of frustration and low self-esteem due to difficulties in accessing educational materials. How can a teacher address Sophie's social/emotional needs?

    A. Provide Sophie with accessible materials in formats like braille or large print, and offer encouragement and support to boost her confidence.

    B. Discourage Sophie from using alternative formats and insist on standardized materials.

    C. Minimize discussions about accessing materials to prevent overwhelming Sophie.

    D. Focus exclusively on academic tasks without considering Sophie's emotional well-being.

Answer:

QUESTION 307

Lucas, a visually impaired student, has shown interest in participating in extracurricular activities, but he's hesitant due to concerns about accessibility. How can a teacher support Lucas's social/emotional development in this situation?

A. Collaborate with relevant stakeholders to ensure that extracurricular activities are accessible to Lucas, and provide encouragement and reassurance.
B. Discourage Lucas from participating in extracurricular activities to avoid potential challenges.
C. Minimize discussions about extracurricular activities to prevent overwhelming Lucas.
D. Focus exclusively on academic tasks without addressing Lucas's interests in extracurriculars.

Answer:

QUESTION 308

In a case study scenario, Sarah, a parent of a visually impaired student, expresses concern about her child's educational progress. What is the first step a teacher can take to support Sarah and her child?

A. Actively listen to Sarah's concerns, validate her feelings, and collaborate on a plan to address her child's needs.
B. Dismiss Sarah's concerns as common worries and reassure her that everything is fine.
C. Minimize discussions about the child's visual impairment to prevent overwhelming Sarah.
D. Provide Sarah with standardized informational materials without personal engagement.

Answer:

QUESTION 309

How can a teacher best support a family whose visually impaired child is transitioning to a new educational setting?

A. Provide information about the new setting, offer opportunities for orientation, and facilitate communication with relevant staff members.
B. Discourage the family from seeking information about the new setting to avoid overwhelming them.
C. Minimize discussions about the transition to prevent potential stress for the family.
D. Assume that the family will handle the transition process independently.

Answer:

QUESTION 310

What is an effective approach to providing counseling and emotional support to families of visually impaired students?

A. Offering a safe and empathetic space for families to express their feelings, concerns, and s, and providing resources or referrals when needed.
B. Avoiding discussions about emotional well-being to maintain a strictly academic focus.
C. Dismissing the emotional aspect of the situation and focusing solely on practical matters.
D. Encouraging families to handle emotional support independently.

Answer:

QUESTION 311

In a case study scenario, Mark, a parent of a visually impaired student, is seeking information on available support networks and resources for families. How can a teacher best assist Mark in this situation?

A. Provide information on local and national support organizations, networks, and resources, and offer assistance in connecting with them.
B. Discourage Mark from seeking outside support, as it may be overwhelming.
C. Minimize discussions about support networks to avoid potential stress for Mark.
D. Assume that Mark will independently find the information he needs.

Answer:

QUESTION 312

Lisa, a mother of a visually impaired student, is concerned about her child's transition to a new school. She's unsure about the available resources and how to best support her child. How can a teacher best assist Lisa in this situation?

A. Offer a meeting to discuss Lisa's concerns, provide information on available resources and services, and guide her through the transition process.
B. Discourage Lisa from seeking additional information to avoid overwhelming her.
C. Minimize discussions about the transition to prevent potential stress for Lisa.
D. Assume that Lisa will independently navigate the transition process.

Answer:

QUESTION 313

John, a father of a visually impaired student, is feeling overwhelmed by the challenges his child faces in the educational setting. How can a teacher best offer support to John?

A. Provide a safe and empathetic space for John to express his feelings, concerns, and s, and offer resources or referrals when needed.
B. Discourage John from discussing his concerns to maintain a strictly academic focus.
C. Minimize discussions about the challenges to prevent potential stress for John.
D. Assume that John will handle his concerns independently.

Answer:

QUESTION 314

Mike, a visually impaired student's parent, is interested in connecting with other families who have children with visual impairments. How can a teacher best assist Mike in finding a supportive network?

A. Provide information on local and national support organizations, networks, and resources, and offer assistance in connecting with them.
B. Discourage Mike from seeking outside support, as it may be overwhelming.
C. Minimize discussions about support networks to avoid potential stress for Mike.
D. Assume that Mike will independently find the support network he needs.

Answer:

QUESTION 315

In a case study scenario, a teacher encounters conflicting research findings regarding the effectiveness of a specific instructional approach for visually impaired students. How should the teacher approach this situation?

  A. Evaluate the quality and source of the research, consider contextual factors, and seek guidance from experts in the field to inform instructional decisions.
  B. Choose an approach based solely on personal preference to maintain consistency in instruction.
  C. Disregard the research findings and rely on traditional teaching methods.
  D. Avoid implementing any approach until more conclusive research is available.

Answer:

QUESTION 316

What is an essential consideration when interpreting research findings for application in the education of visually impaired students?

  A. Recognizing the diversity among visually impaired students and the need for individualized approaches to instruction.
  B. Adopting a one-size-fits-all approach to ensure consistency in instruction.
  C. Disregarding individual differences to maintain uniformity in educational practices.
  D. Minimizing the importance of research in favor of personal teaching preferences.

Answer:

QUESTION 317

In a case study scenario, a teacher encounters a new teaching method supported by recent research. How should the teacher approach the implementation of this method for visually impaired students?

  A. Pilot the new method, closely monitor its effectiveness, and adjust as needed based on ongoing assessment.
  B. Reject the new method to maintain consistency in instruction.
  C. Implement the new method without any modifications based on the research findings alone.
  D. Disregard the new method and continue with established practices.

Answer:

QUESTION 318

What is a critical aspect when applying research findings to instructional practices for visually impaired students?

  A. Ensuring that the research is current, relevant, and aligns with the specific needs and characteristics of the students.
  B. Disregarding research findings in favor of traditional teaching methods.
  C. Implementing research-based practices without consideration for individual student differences.
  D. Minimizing the importance of research in instructional decision-making.

Answer:

QUESTION 319

In a case study scenario, a teacher encounters conflicting research findings regarding the benefits of inclusive education for visually impaired students. How should the teacher approach this situation?

    A. Consider the specific needs and preferences of the visually impaired students, seek input from relevant stakeholders, and weigh the potential benefits and challenges of inclusive education.
    B. Disregard research findings and exclusively rely on traditional teaching methods.
    C. Implement inclusive education practices without further consideration.
    D. Avoid making any changes until more conclusive research is available.

Answer:

QUESTION 320

What role does ongoing professional development play in effectively applying research findings in the education of visually impaired students?

    A. Ongoing professional development allows teachers to stay updated with current research and gain new skills to implement research-based practices effectively.
    B. Professional development is not necessary in applying research findings; teachers can rely on their existing knowledge and practices.
    C. Ongoing professional development may be beneficial, but it is not a significant factor in applying research findings.
    D. Relying solely on initial teacher training is sufficient to apply research findings effectively.

Answer:

QUESTION 321

In a case study scenario, a teacher encounters research suggesting the benefits of using assistive technology for visually impaired students. How should the teacher approach the integration of assistive technology in the classroom?

    A. Explore the specific needs and preferences of each visually impaired student, assess the appropriateness of available assistive technologies, and provide training and support for their effective use.
    B. Avoid integrating assistive technology to maintain consistency in instruction.
    C. Implement assistive technology without further consideration for individual student differences.
    D. Disregard the research findings and continue with established practices.

Answer:

QUESTION 322

Which cognitive skill is essential for visually impaired students to develop efficient orientation and mobility skills, allowing them to navigate their environment safely?

    A. Spatial reasoning
    B. Auditory discrimination
    C. Visual memory
    D. Abstract thinking

Answer:

QUESTION 323

You have a visually impaired student who is struggling with reading braille fluently. Despite consistent practice, their progress is slow. What cognitive skill might be affecting their braille reading ability?

A. Auditory discrimination
B. Tactile perception
C. Visual memory
D. Executive functioning

Answer:

QUESTION 324

What cognitive skill is particularly important for visually impaired students to develop strong problem-solving abilities and adaptability in various situations?

A. Visual memory
B. Auditory discrimination
C. Metacognition
D. Logical reasoning

Answer:

QUESTION 325

A visually impaired student in your class often has difficulty organizing their thoughts when writing essays. What cognitive skill should you focus on to support their writing skills?

A. Auditory memory
B. Attention to detail
C. Executive functioning
D. Visual-spatial skills

Answer:

QUESTION 326

You are an educator responsible for assessing a visually impaired student's academic progress. The standard assessment tools used for the general student population do not consider the student's visual impairment. What is the most appropriate action in this situation?

A. Administer the standard assessment and provide additional time.
B. Adapt the assessment to accommodate the student's visual impairment.
C. Exclude the student from assessment to avoid undue stress.
D. Recommend the student for a different educational program.

Answer:

QUESTION 327

What is the primary purpose of early assessment and intervention for visually impaired students?

  A. Identifying students with the most severe visual impairments
  B. Ensuring that students receive specialized instruction and support
  C. Meeting legal requirements for special education services
  D. Excluding students from general education programs

Answer:

QUESTION 328

A visually impaired student has been consistently struggling with math assessments, despite appropriate accommodations. What should you consider as the next step in addressing their needs?

  A. Conduct a vision assessment to ensure the student's visual impairment hasn't worsened.
  B. Explore alternative methods of math instruction.
  C. Exclude the student from math assessments to reduce stress.
  D. Recommend a change in the student's educational placement.

Answer:

QUESTION 329

What is a key consideration when using standardized assessments for visually impaired students?

  A. Ensuring that the student takes the assessment without any accommodations
  B. Administering the assessment in a separate, quiet room
  C. Adapting the assessment to account for the student's sensory needs
  D. Allowing extra time for the student to complete the assessment

Answer:

QUESTION 330

A visually impaired student's assessment scores consistently fall below grade level. What is the primary goal of assessment in this situation?

  A. Documenting the student's academic challenges for future reference
  B. Determining eligibility for special education services
  C. Assessing the student's eligibility for mainstream classrooms
  D. Identifying the specific learning needs of the student

Answer:

QUESTION 331

What is the significance of using assessments that are nondiscriminatory and culturally fair for visually impaired students?

  A. These assessments help identify students with exceptional talents.
  B. They ensure that visually impaired students have an equal opportunity to succeed.
  C. These assessments provide opportunities for visually impaired students to excel academically.
  D. They are essential for tracking the progress of visually impaired students in special education programs.

Answer:

QUESTION 332

You have a visually impaired student who is proficient in braille and relies on it for reading and writing. The standardized assessments provided by the school are not available in braille format. What should you do to address this issue?

A. Request an exemption from standardized assessments for the student.
B. Provide the assessments orally to the student.
C. Advocate for accessible braille versions of the assessments.
D. Exclude the student from standardized assessments.

Answer:

QUESTION 333

Who is typically responsible for coordinating and leading the Individualized Education Program (IEP) team meetings for a visually impaired student?

A. The school principal
B. The special education teacher
C. The student's parent or guardian
D. The IEP team facilitator

Answer:

QUESTION 334

In an IEP team for a visually impaired student, what is the primary role of the school psychologist?

A. Determining the appropriate placement for the student
B. Conducting assessments to evaluate the student's strengths and needs
C. Developing the student's annual goals and objectives
D. Overseeing the implementation of assistive technology

Answer:

QUESTION 335

An IEP team is discussing the appropriate placement for a visually impaired student. The parent strongly believes that the student should be placed in a mainstream classroom. The special education teacher advocates for a specialized classroom. What should the IEP team prioritize in this situation?

A. Complying with the parent's preference for placement
B. Deciding based on the majority vote of the team members
C. Conducting a comprehensive evaluation of the student's needs and abilities
D. Placing the student in the least restrictive environment (LRE)

Answer:

QUESTION 336

What is the primary role of the speech-language pathologist (SLP) on an IEP team for a visually impaired student?

- A. Conducting vision assessments
- B. Addressing communication and language goals
- C. Ensuring assistive technology is implemented
- D. Coordinating transportation services

Answer:

QUESTION 337

A visually impaired student has recently moved to a new school district. The IEP team is in the process of developing a new IEP. What should the team consider when developing the IEP for this student?

- A. Copying the previous IEP from the student's former district
- B. Conducting a new evaluation to determine current strengths and needs
- C. Placing the student in the same program as their previous school
- D. Including the student in the IEP development process

Answer:

QUESTION 338

What is the primary purpose of the present levels of performance (PLOP) section in an Individualized Education Program (IEP) for a visually impaired student?

- A. Outlining the student's long-term career goals
- B. Identifying the specific accommodations needed for the student
- C. Describing the student's current academic and functional abilities
- D. Defining the roles and responsibilities of IEP team members

Answer:

QUESTION 339

An IEP team is considering the appropriate placement for a visually impaired student. The team is divided, with some members advocating for a mainstream classroom and others for a specialized program. What should be the key guiding principle in making this decision?

- A. The convenience of the school district
- B. The preference of the majority of team members
- C. The best interests and unique needs of the student
- D. Compliance with state education regulations

Answer:

QUESTION 340

You are a special education teacher on an IEP team for a new visually impaired student, Sarah. Sarah's parents insist on placing her in a mainstream classroom, while the school principal recommends a specialized program for visually impaired students. How should the IEP team approach this situation?

A. Follow the principal's recommendation since they have the final say.
B. Comply with the parents' request and place Sarah in a mainstream classroom.
C. Conduct a thorough evaluation to determine the most appropriate placement based on Sarah's needs.
D. Seek legal counsel to resolve the disagreement between the parents and the principal.

Answer:

QUESTION 341

You are an IEP team member for a visually impaired student, Alex. During the IEP meeting, the speech-language pathologist suggests that Alex should receive communication and language therapy twice a week as part of his IEP goals. The parent expresses concern about the additional therapy time interfering with other academic subjects. How should the team address this concern?

A. Follow the speech-language pathologist's recommendation without considering the parent's concerns.
B. Offer the parent an alternative therapy schedule that doesn't conflict with academic subjects.
C. Adjust the therapy frequency based on a mutual agreement between the parent and the IEP team.
D. Remove the communication and language therapy from Alex's IEP to avoid conflicts.

Answer:

QUESTION 342

You are an IEP team member for a visually impaired student, Emily. Emily's previous IEP from her former school district is available, and her parents request that the new IEP mirror the old one. However, Emily has made significant progress since then, and her current abilities differ from those described in the old IEP. How should the IEP team proceed?

A. Use the old IEP as a template and make minimal adjustments to reflect Emily's current status.
B. Disregard the old IEP entirely and start from scratch with a new assessment.
C. Conduct a comprehensive evaluation to determine Emily's current strengths and needs.
D. Agree with the parents' request to keep the old IEP as is, as long as they are comfortable with it.

Answer:

QUESTION 343

You are working with a visually impaired student named Mark who is learning orientation and mobility skills. He is struggling to navigate unfamiliar environments independently. What should be your initial step in addressing Mark's needs effectively?

A. Provide Mark with a white cane and teach him how to use it.
B. Conduct a thorough assessment of Mark's current orientation and mobility skills.
C. Enroll Mark in an orientation and mobility class without further evaluation.
D. Request a meeting with Mark's parents to discuss his challenges.

Answer:

QUESTION 344

What is a critical consideration when selecting adaptive or assistive technologies for a visually impaired student's orientation and mobility training?

- A. The cost-effectiveness of the technology
- B. The popularity and trendiness of the technology
- C. The student's individual needs and preferences
- D. The availability of technical support for the technology

Answer:

QUESTION 345

You have a visually impaired student, Sarah, who is making significant progress in her orientation and mobility skills using a white cane. However, her parents believe that a guide dog would be a better option. What should you consider in this situation?

- A. Immediately transition Sarah to using a guide dog, as her parents prefer.
- B. Conduct an assessment to determine if a guide dog is a suitable option for Sarah.
- C. Ignore the parents' preference and continue with the white cane training.
- D. Consult with a professional dog trainer to assess the feasibility of a guide dog.

Answer:

QUESTION 346

Which of the following is a key factor to consider when adapting instructional methods for teaching orientation and mobility skills to a visually impaired student?

- A. The student's preference for tactile learning materials
- B. The availability of advanced technology solutions
- C. The cost-effectiveness of the adapted methods
- D. The instructor's level of expertise in technology use

Answer:

QUESTION 347

You have a visually impaired student, John, who is proficient in using a white cane for orientation and mobility. He has expressed interest in learning to use a smartphone app designed to assist blind individuals with navigation. What should you do in response to John's request?

- A. Discourage John from using technology and continue with traditional methods.
- B. Provide John with a smartphone and the app without any further evaluation.
- C. Assess John's readiness for using the app and provide appropriate training.
- D. Ignore John's request, as it may not be necessary for his education.

Answer:

QUESTION 348

What is a critical consideration when adapting instructional methods for teaching orientation and mobility skills to a visually impaired student with additional disabilities?

- A. Emphasizing advanced technology solutions
- B. Incorporating multisensory and individualized approaches
- C. Reducing the use of tactile learning materials
- D. Relying solely on traditional methods

Answer:

QUESTION 349

You have a visually impaired student, Maria, who is struggling with using a white cane for navigation due to her limited upper body strength. Her orientation and mobility progress is slow. What should you consider in adapting her instructional methods?

- A. Transition Maria to using a guide dog immediately.
- B. Continue with white cane training without adaptations.
- C. Assess Maria's physical abilities and explore alternative mobility aids.
- D. Provide Maria with additional visual aids to compensate for the cane's limitations.

Answer:

QUESTION 350

You are an orientation and mobility specialist working with a visually impaired student named David, who has limited mobility due to a physical disability. David is eager to learn orientation and mobility skills but faces significant physical challenges. What would be the most appropriate adaptation in this situation?

- A. Introduce David to using a guide dog for mobility.
- B. Continue with traditional white cane training.
- C. Collaborate with a physical therapist to address David's mobility challenges.
- D. Provide David with a GPS navigation device.

Answer:

QUESTION 351

You are an orientation and mobility specialist working with a visually impaired student named Sarah, who is proficient in using a white cane for navigation. Sarah expresses interest in learning to use a smartphone app designed to assist blind individuals with navigation. How should you approach this situation?

- A. Discourage Sarah from using technology and continue with traditional methods.
- B. Provide Sarah with a smartphone and the app without any further evaluation.
- C. Assess Sarah's readiness for using the app and provide appropriate training.
- D. Ignore Sarah's request, as it may not be necessary for her education.

Answer:

QUESTION 352

You have a visually impaired student, James, who has been using a guide dog for orientation and mobility for several years. Recently, James has expressed an interest in learning to use a white cane as an additional mobility aid. How should you proceed with James's request?

A. Encourage James to stick with the guide dog, as it's the most effective option.
B. Provide James with a white cane and minimal instruction, as he's experienced with mobility.
C. Assess James's goals and provide him with comprehensive training on using the white cane.
D. Ignore James's request, as it may confuse his existing mobility skills.

Answer:

QUESTION 353

You have a visually impaired student, Alex, who is struggling with reading and comprehending standard printed textbooks. You want to explore assistive technologies to help him access and understand the content effectively. What should be your initial step in evaluating and selecting appropriate assistive technologies for Alex?

A. Research and select a popular assistive technology tool.
B. Consult with Alex's parents to get their opinion on technology.
C. Conduct an assessment of Alex's specific needs and preferences.
D. Request input from other teachers in the school.

Answer:

QUESTION 354

What is a critical consideration when adapting instructional methods for a visually impaired student with multiple disabilities?

A. Incorporating high-tech assistive technologies
B. Reducing the use of tactile learning materials
C. Focusing primarily on auditory instruction
D. Individualizing instruction based on the student's needs

Answer:

QUESTION 355

You have a visually impaired student, Sarah, who is proficient in using a white cane for mobility. However, she has expressed interest in learning to use a smartphone app designed to assist blind individuals with navigation. How should you address Sarah's request?

A. Discourage Sarah from using technology and continue with traditional methods.
B. Provide Sarah with a smartphone and the app without further evaluation.
C. Assess Sarah's readiness for using the app and provide appropriate training.
D. Ignore Sarah's request, as it may not be necessary for her education.

Answer:

QUESTION 356

What should be a primary consideration when selecting adaptive or assistive technologies for a visually impaired student's individualized instruction?

A. The cost-effectiveness of the technology
B. The availability of technical support for the technology
C. The popularity of the technology among peers
D. The alignment of the technology with the student's educational goals

Answer:

QUESTION 357

You have a visually impaired student, James, who is proficient in using a white cane for mobility. He has expressed interest in learning to use a guide dog as an additional mobility aid. How should you proceed with James's request?

A. Immediately transition James to using a guide dog, as he prefers.
B. Continue with white cane training without adaptations.
C. Assess James's goals and provide him with comprehensive guide dog training.
D. Ignore James's request, as it may be unnecessary for his education.

Answer:

Chapter 2 – Answers and Explanations

QUESTION 1

Answer: B

Explanation: Visually impaired students often experience slower development of gross motor skills compared to their sighted peers, as they may require additional time and practice to develop coordination and spatial awareness without the benefit of visual cues.

QUESTION 2

Answer: B

Explanation: Visually impaired adolescents may experience delayed language acquisition due to reduced exposure to visual stimuli and the need for alternative communication methods such as Braille or sign language, which may take longer to master.

QUESTION 3

Answer: B

Explanation: Visually impaired adolescents may encounter difficulties in abstract thinking and conceptualization, as they may have limited access to visual cues that aid in understanding abstract concepts and relationships.

QUESTION 4

Answer: C

Explanation: Visually impaired adolescents often develop enhanced self-confidence as they learn to navigate their environment and overcome challenges associated with their visual impairment. This increased self-confidence can be a positive aspect of their psychological development.

QUESTION 5

Answer: A

Explanation: The level of familiarity with Braille and the availability of resources for visually impaired individuals can vary across different cultures. This variation can impact the social and emotional development of visually impaired students, as access to Braille materials and educational support may differ significantly.

QUESTION 6

Answer: B

Explanation: The retina, located at the back of the eye, contains specialized cells (rods and cones) responsible for perceiving color (cones) and fine details in the visual field (cones), making it crucial for visual perception.

QUESTION 7

Answer: A

Explanation: Infants usually begin tracking moving objects with their eyes within the first few weeks of life, which is an early milestone in visual development.

QUESTION 8

Answer: D

Explanation: The iris is the colored part of the eye that controls the size of the pupil, regulating the amount of light that enters the eye and aiding in focusing on objects at different distances.

QUESTION 9

Answer: B

Explanation: Children typically refine their ability to perceive and differentiate between colors during early childhood when they become more proficient at identifying and naming various colors.

QUESTION 10

Answer: C

Explanation: The optic nerve carries visual signals from the retina to the brain, allowing for the processing and interpretation of visual information.

QUESTION 11

Answer: C

Explanation: Visual experiences during early childhood, even for children with visual impairments, play a crucial role in establishing cognitive foundations, including spatial understanding and object recognition.

QUESTION 12

Answer: B

Explanation: The lens of the eye helps to focus incoming light onto the retina, allowing for the formation of a clear and focused image for visual perception.

QUESTION 13

Answer: B

Explanation: Visually impaired children often face challenges with spatial orientation and navigation in unfamiliar environments, which can impact their cognitive development, especially in situations where they need to navigate classrooms or school grounds.

QUESTION 14

Answer: B

Explanation: Visual impairment can limit a child's exposure to visual stimuli, which can affect their language development, as they may have less access to visual cues that aid in learning language and vocabulary.

QUESTION 15

Answer: B

Explanation: For a visually impaired student struggling with abstract math concepts, using tactile materials and hands-on activities can help them gain a concrete understanding, as they rely on touch and physical interaction rather than visual cues.

QUESTION 16

Answer: B

Explanation: Visual impairments can lead to delayed development of spatial reasoning skills, as these skills often rely on visual perception, making it a potential challenge for visually impaired children in the context of problem-solving.

QUESTION 17

Answer: C

Explanation: Assistive technology, such as text-to-speech software and Braille displays, can empower visually impaired students to access and interact with written language, supporting their language development and literacy skills.

QUESTION 18

Answer: C

Explanation: To support the participation of a visually impaired student in group discussions, a teacher can provide auditory cues, encourage turn-taking, and create an inclusive classroom environment that accommodates their needs.

QUESTION 19

Answer: C

Explanation: Visual impairments may result in challenges with visual memory tasks, as these tasks often rely on the ability to process and store visual information, which can be limited in visually impaired individuals.

QUESTION 20

Answer: C

Explanation: Braille assessments are specifically designed to evaluate a visually impaired student's proficiency in reading and writing Braille, which is essential for their literacy development.

QUESTION 21

Answer: C

Explanation: Functional vision assessments provide valuable information about a visually impaired student's visual capabilities and limitations, which is essential for determining the most appropriate educational placement and program.

QUESTION 22

Answer: C

Explanation: To monitor the progress of a visually impaired student, it is essential to set clear goals and objectives based on assessment data and then regularly track and adjust these goals to ensure continuous improvement.

QUESTION 23

Answer: C

Explanation: Assessments for visually impaired students primarily aim to determine the degree of visual impairment and its impact on the student's educational needs, allowing for appropriate interventions and support.

QUESTION 24

Answer: B

Explanation: A curriculum-based assessment can help determine the student's specific strengths and weaknesses in the mathematics curriculum, aiding in making targeted placement decisions and developing appropriate interventions.

QUESTION 25

Answer: B

Explanation: Observational assessments, which involve observing the student's behavior and performance in real-life situations, are the most effective way to evaluate compensatory skills like orientation and mobility in visually impaired students.

QUESTION 26

Answer: D

Explanation: To determine the degree of need in compensatory skills areas for a visually impaired student, it is crucial to assess their daily living skills and independence level, as these directly impact their quality of life and educational progress.

QUESTION 27

Answer: B

Explanation: Observational assessments in real-life situations provide a more comprehensive understanding of a visually impaired student's daily living and functional life skills, as they capture the student's performance in authentic contexts.

QUESTION 28

Answer: C

Explanation: To identify specific deficits in fine motor skills, a dedicated fine motor skills assessment is the most appropriate tool, as it focuses on the area of concern.

QUESTION 29

Answer: A

Explanation: The primary goal of assessing communicative competence in a visually impaired student is to identify their primary mode of communication, which can inform appropriate interventions and support.

UESTION 30

Answer: B

Explanation: When assessment results are inconsistent, it is crucial for a special education teacher to consult with other professionals to gain a comprehensive understanding of the student's needs and potential underlying factors.

QUESTION 31

Answer: B

Explanation: An occupational therapy assessment is most valuable for evaluating a visually impaired student's difficulties with daily living skills, as it focuses on practical skills needed for daily life.

QUESTION 32

Answer: C

Explanation: Ongoing assessment is crucial for visually impaired students because it enables educators to track progress, identify changing needs, and make timely adjustments to individualized support and interventions to ensure student success.

QUESTION 33

Answer: C

Explanation: When communicating assessment results to parents, the primary focus should be on highlighting the student's strengths and areas for improvement, which can guide discussions about support and interventions.

QUESTION 34

Answer: B

Explanation: In this case, Sarah's difficulty in navigating the classroom suggests a potential problem with her orientation and mobility skills. An orientation and mobility assessment is designed to evaluate her ability to navigate her environment safely and independently, making it the most appropriate assessment to address her specific issue.

QUESTION 35

Answer: C

Explanation: A functional vision assessment is specifically designed to evaluate how a student's visual impairment affects their daily functioning, including reading and writing tasks. It is the most appropriate assessment approach to identify Mark's specific needs related to his visual impairment.

QUESTION 36

Answer: D

Explanation: For assessing Emma's progress and making adjustments to her communication support, implementing ongoing assessment through regular observations and data collection is the most effective strategy. This approach allows her teacher to track her progress over time and make targeted interventions as needed, which is particularly valuable for students with special needs like Emma.

QUESTION 37

Answer: B

Explanation: The level of family support and involvement plays a critical role in the development of orientation and mobility skills in visually impaired students. Families who actively support and encourage these skills can significantly enhance a student's confidence and ability to navigate their environment.

QUESTION 38

Answer: C

Explanation: To help visually impaired students achieve orientation and mobility goals, it is crucial to encourage independent problem-solving and decision-making skills. This strategy promotes self-reliance and enhances their ability to navigate various real-world environments safely.

QUESTION 39

Answer: B

Explanation: Overreliance on technology for navigation can potentially reduce a student's problem-solving skills, as they may become less inclined to explore alternative solutions or strategies when faced with navigation challenges.

QUESTION 40

Answer: C

Explanation: Incorporating real-world environments into orientation and mobility training helps visually impaired students generalize their skills, making them better equipped to navigate a wide range of settings and situations.

QUESTION 41

Answer: C

Explanation: A strong desire for independence and the opportunity for socialization can motivate visually impaired students to develop orientation and mobility skills, as these skills enable them to participate more fully in social activities and daily life.

QUESTION 42

Answer: C

Explanation: Designing effective learning experiences for orientation and mobility requires tailoring instruction to meet the individual needs and goals of each visually impaired student, recognizing that their abilities and objectives may vary.

QUESTION 43

Answer: B

Explanation: The age and developmental stage of the student are primary factors in assessing readiness for orientation and mobility training, as the content and methods of instruction should align with the student's developmental level and abilities.

QUESTION 44

Answer: C

Explanation: To support Alex's desire to participate in sports, it is essential to provide orientation and mobility training that is tailored to his specific sports interests. This approach will empower him to develop the necessary skills to engage safely and independently in his chosen extracurricular activities.

QUESTION 45

Answer: C

Explanation: To help Emily improve her orientation and mobility skills within the school environment, it is essential to implement a structured orientation and mobility program. This program can provide her with the necessary training and support to navigate the school independently and safely.

QUESTION 46

Answer: C

Explanation: To prepare Jacob for his transition to a music conservatory in a new city, it is important to offer orientation and mobility training specifically focused on urban navigation skills. This will equip him with the skills and confidence needed to navigate the city independently and pursue his career aspirations.

QUESTION 47

Answer: B

Explanation: Adapting materials and methods to accommodate the specific needs of a visually impaired student is a critical consideration when planning the curriculum. This ensures that the student can access and engage with the content effectively.

QUESTION 48

Answer: B

Explanation: Using tactile materials and hands-on activities is a key strategy to promote concept development in mathematics for visually impaired students. These methods allow students to explore mathematical concepts through touch and physical engagement, enhancing their understanding.

QUESTION 49

Answer: A

Explanation: One potential challenge in developing a curriculum for visually impaired students in science is the lack of accessible science textbooks and resources. Ensuring that science materials are available in accessible formats is crucial to their success in the subject.

QUESTION 50

Answer: B

Explanation: Involving visually impaired students in hands-on, experiential learning activities enhances their problem-solving and critical thinking abilities. These activities encourage active engagement and deeper understanding of academic concepts.

QUESTION 51

Answer: D

Explanation: When developing the curriculum for a visually impaired student in social studies, a primary focus should be on adapting materials to ensure accessibility and comprehension. This ensures that the student can access and understand the content effectively.

QUESTION 52

Answer: C

Explanation: Encouraging visually impaired students to develop and use study routines is a key strategy for promoting study skills. Establishing effective study habits and routines can enhance their academic success and independence.

QUESTION 53

Answer: C

Explanation: A critical factor in developing the curriculum for a visually impaired student in reading/language arts is adapting materials to address individual reading levels and interests. This approach ensures that the student can engage with materials that are both accessible and relevant to their needs and abilities.

QUESTION 54

Answer: B

Explanation: To support Maria's interest in science, the best approach is to modify existing materials to make them accessible to her. This can be done by incorporating tactile diagrams and providing descriptions to ensure she can actively participate in hands-on experiments.

QUESTION 55

Answer: C

Explanation: To facilitate Daniel's involvement in literary studies, the best approach is to collaborate with the school to obtain or create accessible versions of the literary texts he wishes to study. This ensures that he has equal access to the curriculum.

QUESTION 56

Answer: B

Explanation: To help Sophia excel in mathematics, it is crucial to modify the curriculum by incorporating tactile materials and providing verbal descriptions of mathematical concepts. This approach ensures that she can access and engage with the subject effectively.

QUESTION 57

Answer: C

Explanation: When evaluating and selecting instructional strategies and materials for visually impaired students, the primary consideration should be tailoring instruction to meet the unique needs of each student. This individualization promotes effective learning.

QUESTION 58

Answer: B

Explanation: For a visually impaired student pursuing a career in computer programming, screen readers and screen magnification software are essential assistive technologies. These tools enable access to computer code and programming languages.

QUESTION 59

Answer: B

Explanation: A primary consideration when selecting adaptive or assistive technologies should be cost-effectiveness and adherence to budget constraints. Ensuring that the chosen technologies are financially sustainable is crucial for educational programs.

QUESTION 60

Answer: C

Explanation: A critical step in adapting instructional materials for visually impaired students is modifying the materials to be accessible in alternative formats, such as Braille, large print, or digital formats. This ensures equitable access to the content.

QUESTION 61

Answer: A

Explanation: A key consideration when evaluating community resources for vocational/career competence is the alignment of resources with the student's personal interests and preferences. Tailoring resources to the student's goals is essential for success.

QUESTION 62

Answer: B

Explanation: Braille music notation materials are the most suitable adaptive resource for John's pursuit of a musical career. These materials allow him to read and understand musical notation independently.

QUESTION 63

Answer: C

Explanation: A primary goal when adapting instructional strategies for visually impaired students is to ensure that the strategies align with the student's individual learning preferences and needs, promoting effective learning and engagement.

QUESTION 64

Answer: C

Explanation: An essential ethical consideration is respecting the individual needs and preferences of visually impaired students. Special education teachers must tailor their approach to meet each student's unique requirements.

QUESTION 65

Answer: B

Explanation: In this case, the ethical responsibility is to advocate for the student's needs and explore funding options or alternatives to ensure that the student has access to necessary assistive technology.

QUESTION 66

Answer: C

Explanation: A significant legal requirement is ensuring that all students, including those with visual impairments, receive a free and appropriate public education (FAPE) as mandated by federal law.

QUESTION 67

Answer: C

Explanation: Special education teachers have a critical legal obligation to maintain the privacy and confidentiality of student records in compliance with laws such as the Family Educational Rights and Privacy Act (FERPA).

QUESTION 68

Answer: B

Explanation: Ethically and professionally, the first step should be to schedule a meeting with the parent to discuss their concerns, gather information, and collaborate on addressing any issues.

QUESTION 69

Answer: C

Explanation: Teachers of students with visual impairments should determine assessment accommodations based on individual student needs and the specific requirements of each assessment.

QUESTION 70

Answer: B

Explanation: In this situation, the ethical and professional response is to advocate for the student's IEP recommendations and seek appropriate funding to ensure that the student's needs are met in accordance with the law.

QUESTION 71

Answer: A

Explanation: Visual impairment can significantly affect a student's cognitive development as it may impact their ability to perceive and process visual information, which plays a crucial role in learning, problem-solving, and understanding the world around them.

QUESTION 72

Answer: A

Explanation: Visual impairment can pose challenges in social development since it may limit opportunities for observing and engaging in visual social cues and interactions, which are important for the development of social skills and relationships.

QUESTION 73

Answer: A

Explanation: Braille instruction is a critical strategy for fostering development in visually impaired students, as it directly supports their literacy and cognitive development, which, in turn, impacts other domains such as communication, social interaction, and academic achievement.

QUESTION 74

Answer: B

Explanation: Engaging visually impaired students in physical activities not only promotes physical development but also enhances their spatial awareness, coordination, and overall well-being. It allows them to explore their environment and build confidence in their physical abilities.

QUESTION 75

Answer: B

Explanation: Congenital blindness is typically caused by genetic factors or conditions that occur during fetal development, leading to visual impairment from birth. Understanding the causes of congenital blindness is crucial for special education teachers to tailor their support and instruction effectively.

QUESTION 76

Answer: A

Explanation: Visual acuity refers to the sharpness of vision and the ability to see fine details. Impairments in visual acuity can significantly affect a student's reading and ability to interpret visual information, making it a critical consideration for educators.

QUESTION 77

Answer: C

Explanation: Hemianopia is a visual impairment characterized by a loss of vision in half of the visual field, which can affect a student's ability to detect objects or information on the side, emphasizing the importance of adapting teaching materials accordingly.

QUESTION 78

Answer: B

Explanation: Nystagmus is a visual condition characterized by involuntary eye movements, which can make it challenging for students to maintain visual focus. Educators should be aware of this condition when planning instructional strategies.

QUESTION 79

Answer: D

Explanation: Strabismus is a visual impairment characterized by misalignment of the eyes, which can lead to double vision and difficulties in perceiving depth accurately. Teachers should consider the impact of strabismus on a student's visual experience.

QUESTION 80

Answer: B

Explanation: Retinal degeneration is a condition where the cells in the retina deteriorate over time, resulting in a gradual loss of central vision. Special education teachers should be aware of this condition as it can impact a student's ability to read and access visual information.

QUESTION 81

Answer: D

Explanation: Color blindness is a visual impairment that affects an individual's ability to distinguish between certain colors. Teachers should consider this condition when designing materials and activities to ensure accessibility for visually impaired students.

QUESTION 82

Answer: B

Explanation: Visual impairment often requires students to rely more on auditory input for learning, including comprehension. Addressing auditory processing needs can help the student better understand and retain information presented orally.

QUESTION 83

Answer: A

Explanation: Metacognition, or the ability to think about and monitor one's own thinking processes, is crucial for visually impaired students when using language. It helps them plan, organize, and evaluate their communication effectively.

QUESTION 84

Answer: B

Explanation: Pragmatic language skills involve the use of language in social contexts, including turn-taking, topic maintenance, and understanding nonverbal cues. Focusing on pragmatics can help the student improve their social communication.

QUESTION 85

Answer: C

Explanation: To address Sophia's concerns and ensure her continued access to technology, it is important to collaborate with specialists to assess and potentially upgrade the refreshable braille display, ensuring it meets her current needs.

QUESTION 86

Answer: B

Explanation: Promoting self-reliance and autonomy is essential in helping visually impaired students develop independent living skills.

QUESTION 87

Answer: B

Explanation: To support the student's interest in playing a musical instrument, providing opportunities for adapted music lessons and materials can be an effective approach.

QUESTION 88

Answer: C

Explanation: Enhancing transition readiness involves providing students with opportunities to explore vocational and career options as part of their post-school planning.

QUESTION 89

Answer: B

Explanation: To support the student's interest in computer programming, providing access to appropriate courses and assistive technology can help them pursue their career goals effectively.

QUESTION 90

Answer: B

Explanation: Self-advocacy is crucial for enhancing transition readiness as it empowers students to communicate their needs, preferences, and career goals effectively.

QUESTION 91

Answer: C

Explanation: Preparing visually impaired students for post-school life should involve providing opportunities for skill development and practical experiences that enhance transition readiness.

QUESTION 92

Answer: C

Explanation: Learning experiences to enhance transition readiness should be tailored to the individual interests, goals, and needs of visually impaired students, ensuring a personalized and effective transition plan.

QUESTION93:

Answer: B

Explanation: To support Alex's goal of learning to cook independently, providing resources for accessible cooking lessons outside of school can help him acquire this essential skill.

QUESTION 94

Answer: B

Explanation: To support Sarah's interest in a career in graphic design, providing information and resources on graphic design programs and internships can help her explore and pursue her career aspirations.

QUESTION 95

Answer: B

Explanation: To empower David to address concerns about the accessibility of university resources, teaching him about self-advocacy and how to request accessible materials will enable him to effectively advocate for his needs. This skill is vital for a smooth transition to university.

QUESTION 96

Answer: C

Explanation: Collaboration with relevant agencies and professionals is essential to ensure that the unique needs of visually impaired students are met effectively.

QUESTION 97

Answer: C

Explanation: Collaborating with orientation and mobility specialists is essential to develop a tailored training plan to help the student navigate the community independently.

QUESTION 98

Answer: B

Explanation: Establishing positive relationships with community institutions allows schools to leverage community resources, providing students with valuable support and opportunities during the transition process.

QUESTION 99

Answer: C

Explanation: To facilitate the student's vocational training, establishing contacts with the trade school and exploring enrollment options is a proactive step to support their transition.

QUESTION 100

Answer: C

Explanation: Involving community institutions and resources in transition planning enhances students' access to opportunities and support, increasing the likelihood of successful post-school outcomes.

QUESTION 101

Answer: C

Explanation: Establishing relationships with community institutions should focus on leveraging community resources to meet the individualized needs of visually impaired students during their transition.

QUESTION 102

Answer: C

Explanation: Ongoing communication and collaboration with community institutions are essential to ensure that visually impaired students have access to the services and opportunities needed for a successful transition to post-school life.

QUESTION 103

Answer: B

Explanation: To ensure that Lisa receives the necessary technology, exploring partnerships with organizations that provide assistive technology is a proactive step to meet her needs effectively.

QUESTION 104

Answer: C

Explanation: To facilitate David's participation, establishing communication with the league and exploring accommodations is essential to ensure his inclusion and access to recreational activities.

QUESTION 105

Answer: B

Explanation: When adapting instructional methods for teaching visually impaired students with additional disabilities, incorporating multisensory and individualized approaches is crucial. These approaches can address the unique learning needs and preferences of each student, maximizing their learning potential.

QUESTION 106

Answer: C

Explanation: In this scenario, it's essential to assess Emma's current abilities and adapt instruction based on her specific needs. Emma's changing vision requires a tailored approach to ensure she receives the appropriate support and resources.

QUESTION 107

Answer: C

Explanation: To support Michael's interest in guide dog training, it's crucial to assess his goals and readiness and provide appropriate guidance. This approach ensures that the decision aligns with his needs and preferences.

QUESTION 108

Answer: C

Explanation: To make an informed decision, it's essential to assess Ethan's specific needs and abilities to determine if a screen reader is suitable. This assessment ensures that the technology aligns with his individualized instruction and supports his learning effectively.

QUESTION 109

Answer: C

Explanation: In this scenario, it's crucial to collaborate with Emily's classroom teacher to assess Emily's specific needs and discuss strategies for providing appropriate materials. Effective collaboration and communication with the classroom teacher are essential to address the issue.

QUESTION 110

Answer: B

Explanation: When providing training to teachers individually, it's essential to tailor the training to each teacher's specific needs and challenges related to supporting visually impaired students. Personalized training is more effective in addressing their unique circumstances.

QUESTION 111

Answer: C

Explanation: Collaborating with Daniel's physical education teacher to develop tailored strategies is essential to ensure that he can participate effectively in physical activities. This approach promotes teamwork and problem-solving to support Daniel's inclusion.

QUESTION 112

Answer: B

Explanation: Regular and effective communication with other teaching professionals is critical when coordinating instruction for visually impaired students. This communication ensures that everyone is aligned in their approach, leading to better support for the student's needs.

QUESTION 113

Answer: C

Explanation: Collaborating with the regular classroom teacher to develop strategies for integrating braille into lessons is a productive approach. It promotes teamwork and ensures that Ava's specific needs are met within the inclusive classroom setting.

QUESTION 114

Answer: C

Explanation: Collaborating with Leo's classroom teacher to assess his mobility skills and develop safety strategies is essential. This approach ensures that Leo can navigate the school environment independently while addressing safety concerns.

QUESTION 115

Answer: C

Explanation: Collaborating with Max's classroom teacher to identify suitable assistive technology solutions is the most effective approach. It allows for teamwork and ensures that the technology selected aligns with Max's needs and can be integrated into the regular classroom environment.

QUESTION 116

Answer: D

Explanation: Developing a flexible classroom routine that combines group and individual instruction allows you to address the needs of all your visually impaired students effectively. This approach promotes inclusivity and ensures that each student receives the appropriate level of support.

QUESTION 117

Answer: C

Explanation: When applying special education-related regulations and guidelines, particularly concerning equity and program development, it is essential to ensure that individualized plans and accommodations are in place to address each visually impaired student's unique needs. Equity is achieved by providing tailored support.

QUESTION 118

Answer: C

Explanation: Collaborating with the school's assessment coordinator to create a coordinated assessment schedule is the most efficient way to manage assessments for visually impaired students. This approach ensures that assessments are scheduled in an organized and timely manner.

QUESTION 119

Answer: C

Explanation: A crucial aspect of applying special education-related regulations and guidelines is providing accommodations and modifications to ensure that visually impaired students have equal access and opportunities in educational settings. This supports their learning and participation.

QUESTION 120

Answer: A

Explanation: Visually impaired students often rely on their auditory senses as the primary modality for acquiring information and learning. They use their sense of hearing to gather information from the environment, including spoken language, sounds, and verbal instructions.

QUESTION 121

Answer: C

Explanation: Scaffolding involves providing support and guidance to students based on their current abilities. For visually impaired students, this often includes verbal explanations and assistance to help them learn and progress effectively.

QUESTION 122

Answer: D

Explanation: Learning Braille involves a sensorimotor process where students develop tactile recognition and motor skills to read and write using raised dots. This process is critical for visually impaired students.

QUESTION 123

Answer: B

Explanation: UDL promotes flexible teaching methods that cater to diverse learner needs. For visually impaired students, offering a variety of sensory options (e.g., auditory, tactile) and instructional approaches ensures inclusive learning experiences.

QUESTION 124

Answer: C

Explanation: Social Learning Theory, developed by Albert Bandura, emphasizes the role of observation and imitation in the learning process. Visually impaired students can benefit from this theory by learning from others through verbal descriptions and tactile exploration.

QUESTION 125

Answer: A

Explanation: Avoiding activities that require close-up visual tasks, such as reading or drawing, could be a sign that a student is experiencing difficulty with their vision and may have a visual impairment.

QUESTION 126

Answer: A

Explanation: Squinting or tilting the head can indicate difficulty in seeing objects up close, which is a common behavior associated with near-sightedness.

QUESTION 127

Answer: D

Explanation: Nystagmus is a condition characterized by involuntary eye movements, which can lead to difficulty focusing on objects and result in bumping into things.

QUESTION 128

Answer: B

Explanation: Holding objects very close to the face can be a sign of hyperopia, a condition where distant objects appear blurred while close objects can be seen more clearly.

QUESTION 129

Answer: B

Explanation: Strabismus, also known as crossed eyes, can lead to poor hand-eye coordination and difficulties with depth perception.

QUESTION 130

Answer: C

Explanation: Astigmatism can cause blurred or distorted vision, making it challenging for a student to maintain their place while reading.

QUESTION 131

Answer: D

Explanation: Frequently turning the head to the side may suggest a visual impairment that affects peripheral vision, such as retinitis pigmentosa or visual field loss.

QUESTION 132

Answer: A

Explanation: Visual impairments can impact a student's ability to perceive and engage with peers, potentially leading to frustration and social withdrawal during group activities.

QUESTION 133

Answer: C

Explanation: Visual impairments can affect a student's sense of balance and spatial orientation, requiring additional support to ensure safe mobility.

QUESTION 134

Answer: A

Explanation: Developing cooking and meal preparation skills is essential for students with visual impairments to enhance their daily living and functional independence.

QUESTION 135

Answer: B

Explanation: Peer support can help reduce feelings of frustration and anxiety in students with visual impairments, providing them with emotional support and a sense of belonging.

QUESTION 136

Answer: C

Explanation: Effective communication skills are crucial for students with visual impairments in a professional context, enabling them to interact with colleagues, clients, and employers.

QUESTION 137

Answer: C

Explanation: Occupational therapists specialize in helping individuals, including those with visual impairments, develop skills for daily living and functional independence, such as dressing.

QUESTION 138

Answer: B

Explanation: Visual impairments can sometimes lead to a fear of social interactions due to challenges in perceiving and engaging with others visually. This is a common social/emotional challenge for such students.

QUESTION 139

Answer: C

Explanation: Visual acuity (clarity of vision) and visual field (the area a person can see) are key characteristics assessed during formal vision assessments to determine a student's visual abilities.

QUESTION 140

Answer: B

Explanation: An informal functional vision assessment can help identify specific issues, such as difficulties in tracking Braille, and inform strategies for improvement.

QUESTION 141

Answer: C

Explanation: Visual acuity measures the clarity and sharpness of a person's vision, typically assessed by reading letters or symbols on an eye chart.

QUESTION 142

Answer: C

Explanation: An informal functional vision assessment can provide detailed insights into specific challenges like tracking moving objects, helping to tailor interventions.

QUESTION 143

Answer: B

Explanation: Ongoing assessment of visual behavior involves tracking changes in a student's visual abilities and needs as they develop or in response to interventions.

QUESTION 144

Answer: C

Explanation: Ongoing assessment is suitable for tracking changes and progression in a student's visual condition over an extended period.

QUESTION 145

Answer: A

Explanation: Visual field refers to the area a person can see while looking straight ahead without moving their eyes, and it is assessed to determine the extent of a student's visual field.

QUESTION 146

Answer: B

Explanation: Sarah's behavior suggests specific difficulties related to reading. An informal functional vision assessment would help identify and address her specific visual challenges in reading, such as tracking or visual acuity issues.

QUESTION 147

Answer: C

Explanation: Mark's challenges may be related to changes in his visual abilities. An ongoing assessment of visual behavior would help monitor and address these changes over time.

QUESTION 148

Answer: C

Explanation: Emily's difficulties may require ongoing assessment to understand her specific visual behavior challenges and develop appropriate interventions. This approach is more comprehensive than a one-time vision screening.

QUESTION 149

Answer: A

Explanation: The PLAAFP section of an IEP provides a detailed assessment of the student's current performance levels and serves as the foundation for setting annual goals and objectives.

QUESTION 150

Answer: C

Explanation: The annual goals and objectives in an IEP define specific, measurable targets that the student is expected to achieve within a set timeframe.

QUESTION 151

Answer: D

Explanation: For Rachel's IEP to address her orientation and mobility needs, it should include specific goals related to these skills to ensure her safety and independence.

QUESTION 152

Answer: D

Explanation: To evaluate progress, it's essential to gather data and evidence that demonstrate how the student is performing in relation to their IEP goals and objectives.

QUESTION 153

Answer: B

Explanation: If a student is not making sufficient progress, the IEP team should consider modifying the goals and objectives to better suit the student's needs and abilities.

QUESTION 154

Answer: C

Explanation: When a student has achieved their current goals, the IEP team should consider setting new, more challenging goals to continue supporting their growth and development.

QUESTION 155

Answer: C

Explanation: The Special Education Services and Supports section of an IEP outlines the specific accommodations, services, and supports that the student will receive to help them achieve their goals and objectives.

QUESTION 156

Answer: D

Explanation: In this case, it's essential to modify the IEP goals to address Alex's changing vision and ensure that his goals remain relevant and attainable based on his current abilities.

QUESTION 157

Answer: C

Explanation: Instead of reducing support, the IEP team should set new, more challenging goals in Sarah's areas of strength to continue her growth and development.

QUESTION 158

Answer: B

Explanation: If James is not making progress, the IEP team should consider modifying his goals and objectives to better address his specific challenges and needs, rather than discontinuing services or reducing meeting frequency.

QUESTION 159

Answer: B

Explanation: Tactile discrimination skills can be enhanced by using textured materials and objects, allowing students to explore and differentiate through touch.

QUESTION 160

Answer: C

Explanation: Tactile shape puzzles can help Emma improve her ability to recognize and differentiate common objects by touch through hands-on exploration.

QUESTION 161

Answer: C

Explanation: To support sensory training for visually impaired students, it's essential to provide access to both tactile and auditory information and materials.

QUESTION 162

Answer: D

Explanation: A digital image-to-text converter would allow Michael to access descriptions or explanations of famous artworks, enabling him to learn about them despite his visual impairment.

QUESTION 163

Answer: B

Explanation: The selection of adaptive and assistive technologies should align with the specific sensory training needs of the individual student for optimal effectiveness.

QUESTION 164

Answer: C

Explanation: A hearing aid with noise cancellation can enhance Julia's auditory processing and comprehension during sensory training by reducing background noise and improving clarity.

QUESTION 165

Answer: B

Explanation: Adaptive and assistive technologies are used to provide visually impaired students with alternative sensory experiences and enhance their learning opportunities through tactile, auditory, or other means.

QUESTION 166

Answer: C

Explanation: Jordan's reluctance indicates a need for a supportive approach. The teacher should create a safe environment and introduce textures gradually, allowing Jordan to build confidence and tactile discrimination skills over time.

QUESTION 167

Answer: B

Explanation: A digital screen reader can convert visual content, such as diagrams, into auditory or tactile information, allowing Maria to access science concepts through her preferred sensory channel.

QUESTION 168

Answer: C

Explanation: To address David's concerns and improve his mobility skills, it's essential to provide a supportive and controlled environment for stair practice, ensuring his safety and confidence in the process.

QUESTION 169

Answer: C

Explanation: Social development in visually impaired students is enhanced by providing opportunities for peer interactions and friendships, helping them build social skills and relationships.

QUESTION 170

Answer: B

Explanation: A strengths-based counseling approach emphasizes a student's abilities and strengths, which can help Sarah develop a positive self-concept despite her visual impairment.

QUESTION 171

Answer: C

Explanation: Facilitating self-determination involves encouraging students to make choices, set goals, and have a say in their own decisions and plans.

QUESTION 172

Answer: B

Explanation: Role-playing assertive communication scenarios can help Alex practice and develop assertiveness skills in a supportive and controlled setting.

QUESTION 173

Answer: B

Explanation: Practicing active listening and empathy allows teachers to understand students' emotional needs and support their social development effectively.

QUESTION 174

Answer: B

Explanation: Collaborating with other professionals allows for a comprehensive approach to addressing James's social adjustment challenges, involving multiple perspectives and strategies.

QUESTION 175

Answer: C

Explanation: Creating a safe and supportive environment allows visually impaired students to express their emotions and seek emotional support when needed.

QUESTION 176

Answer: C

Explanation: To support Emily's social development, it's essential to facilitate opportunities for her to interact with peers and provide coaching on social skills to help her build relationships.

QUESTION 177

Answer: C

Explanation: A strengths-based counseling approach can help Mark build confidence and assertiveness by emphasizing his abilities and encouraging him to communicate assertively.

QUESTION 178

Answer: B

Explanation: Collaborating with other professionals allows for a comprehensive approach to addressing Sarah's social adjustment challenges, involving multiple perspectives and strategies to support her adaptation in the new school.

QUESTION 179

Answer: C

Explanation: Effective communication with families, including those from diverse backgrounds, involves creating an open and respectful environment that is culturally sensitive to the needs and preferences of each family.

QUESTION 180

Answer: C

Explanation: Using bilingual staff or interpreters can bridge the language gap and facilitate effective communication with Maria's parents, ensuring their active participation in her education.

QUESTION 181

Answer: C

Explanation: To promote family participation, it's crucial to view families as equal partners in planning and implementing their child's education, valuing their input and preferences.

QUESTION 182

Answer: C

Explanation: To engage busy parents like John's, it's essential to offer flexible meeting times and explore alternative communication methods, such as virtual meetings or written updates, to accommodate their schedules.

QUESTION 183

Answer: C

Explanation: Open and regular communication with parents is vital for promoting their active involvement in their child's education, allowing for the exchange of information and collaboration.

QUESTION 184

Answer: C

Explanation: To ensure effective communication with a family with limited technology access, Lisa should use a variety of communication methods, including non-digital options such as phone calls or written communication.

QUESTION 185

Answer: C

Explanation: Open, honest, and transparent communication is essential for establishing trust and positive relationships with families, allowing for productive collaboration in their child's education.

QUESTION 186

Answer: A

Explanation: Respecting and acknowledging cultural differences is crucial. The teacher should encourage open dialogue, respect their beliefs, and find ways to collaborate effectively while considering their cultural background.

QUESTION 187

Answer: C

Explanation: To effectively communicate and collaborate with Mark's family, the teacher should adapt communication styles and approaches to be culturally sensitive and respectful of their diverse background.

QUESTION 188

Answer: C

Explanation: To ensure active involvement of busy parents like Alex's, the teacher should offer flexible meeting times and explore alternative communication methods that accommodate their schedules and preferences, fostering their participation in their child's education.

QUESTION 189

Answer: C

Explanation: Over time, the historical foundation of special education for visually impaired students has evolved to promote inclusive education and the integration of these students into mainstream educational settings.

QUESTION 190

Answer: B

Explanation: A current trend is the advancement of accessible technologies and materials, which can significantly support visually impaired students like Emily in accessing educational content.

QUESTION 191

Answer: B

Explanation: The philosophical foundation of special education for visually impaired students is based on the principle of providing equal educational opportunities and access to education.

QUESTION 192

Answer: B

Explanation: A current issue in the field is the high cost and limited availability of assistive technology devices, which can present challenges for students like Mark in accessing these tools.

QUESTION 193

Answer: B

Explanation: The social model of disability is a significant theoretical foundation that promotes inclusivity, accessibility, and support for visually impaired students within education.

QUESTION 194

Answer: C

Explanation: A current trend is the advancement of inclusive education practices and accessibility measures to support the inclusion of visually impaired students in mainstream classrooms.

QUESTION 195

Answer: C

Explanation: A current trend is the advancement of digital and online alternatives for educational content to enhance access and flexibility for visually impaired students.

QUESTION 196

Answer: C

Explanation: Visually impaired students often require assistive technology to access educational materials, and the lack of such technology can impede their learning.

QUESTION 197

Answer: B

Explanation: Tactile graphics and braille materials are essential tools for visually impaired students to access information effectively.

QUESTION 198

Answer: C

Explanation: Lack of awareness and understanding about visual impairment can create social and educational barriers for visually impaired students.

QUESTION 199

Answer: B

Explanation: Clear verbal instructions and descriptions are essential for conveying information effectively to visually impaired students.

QUESTION 200

Answer: C

Explanation: Group activities and collaboration can help visually impaired students develop social skills and enhance their learning experiences by working with peers.

QUESTION 201

Answer: C

Explanation: To support visually impaired students effectively, it's crucial to tailor instruction and support to their unique needs and abilities.

QUESTION 202

Answer: C

Explanation: Promoting a growth mindset involves praising students' efforts and emphasizing that their abilities can improve through dedication and hard work.

QUESTION 203

Answer: C

Explanation: Assessment should be diverse and consider various ways to evaluate the learning of visually impaired students, taking into account their individual needs and abilities.

QUESTION 204

Answer: B

Explanation: Self-advocacy is crucial for visually impaired students as it helps them express their needs, preferences, and accommodations, promoting independence and effective learning.

QUESTION 205

Answer: C

Explanation: Understanding the significance of disabilities for learning allows educators to provide individualized support and accommodations to meet the specific needs of visually impaired students.

QUESTION 206

Answer: C

Explanation: Collaborative partnerships with families create a supportive network that can contribute to the success and well-being of visually impaired students by sharing insights and support.

QUESTION 207

Answer: C

Explanation: To facilitate learning, educators should prioritize adapting materials into accessible formats, such as braille or tactile graphics, to meet the needs of visually impaired students.

QUESTION 208

Answer: C

Explanation: Proper training and guidance are crucial when teaching visually impaired students to use low vision aids effectively.

QUESTION 209

Answer: B

Explanation: In such a situation, the teacher should offer support and strategies to help the student use the low vision aid in a challenging environment.

QUESTION 210

Answer: B

Explanation: The severity of the visual impairment is a crucial factor in determining whether low vision aids are appropriate for a student.

QUESTION 211

Answer: C

Explanation: Low vision aids should be used when they improve a visually impaired student's access to information and enhance their learning experience.

QUESTION 212

Answer: B

Explanation: The teacher should consider providing alternative methods for the student to participate in art if using low vision aids is challenging.

QUESTION 213

Answer: C

Explanation: Introducing low vision aids should involve clear instruction and guided practice to ensure the student understands how to use them effectively.

QUESTION 214

Answer: B

Explanation: Collaboration with vision specialists can offer valuable expertise and insights to help determine the appropriateness of low vision aids for a student, taking into account their specific needs and options available.

QUESTION 215

Answer: C

Explanation: Understanding how the visual impairment affects the student's learning is a crucial aspect of interpreting assessment results.

QUESTION 216

Answer: B

Explanation: Visual acuity measurements can help in tailoring instructional strategies to meet the student's visual needs effectively.

QUESTION 217

Answer: C

Explanation: Assessment results should guide the development of individualized and targeted instruction that addresses the specific needs of the visually impaired student.

QUESTION 218

Answer: C

Explanation: Collaborating with medical specialists and educators can provide a more comprehensive understanding of the assessment results and inform appropriate interventions.

QUESTION 219

Answer: C

Explanation: The teacher should use assessment results to develop strategies that support the development of visual-motor skills.

QUESTION 220

Answer: B

Explanation: Making assumptions based solely on assessment scores can lead to inaccurate judgments about the student's abilities and needs.

QUESTION 221

Answer: C

Explanation: Interpreting assessment results helps in tailoring individualized support and interventions that address the specific needs of visually impaired students, promoting their learning and development.

QUESTION 222

Answer: C

Explanation: Modifying the learning environment for visually impaired students should involve individualized accommodations tailored to each student's specific needs.

QUESTION 223

Answer: B

Explanation: In such a scenario, it's essential to provide accessible alternatives to printed materials to ensure the student's access to the curriculum.

QUESTION 224

Answer: B

Explanation: Collaborating with healthcare professionals is crucial for providing specialized care and management for students with physical and health impairments.

QUESTION 225

Answer: C

Explanation: Designing an inclusive classroom environment for students with mobility challenges involves incorporating ramps and accessible seating to ensure equal access.

QUESTION 226

Answer: C

Explanation: The goal of management strategies is to create an inclusive environment that maximizes learning time and fosters positive behavior for all students.

QUESTION 227

Answer: B

Explanation: Collaborating with specialists can help identify and address the underlying causes of disruptive behavior in a visually impaired student.

QUESTION 228

Answer: B

Explanation: Positive reinforcement helps create a positive and supportive classroom environment, fostering better behavior and learning outcomes for visually impaired students.

QUESTION229:

Answer: B

Explanation: To support Sarah's inclusion and learning, providing accessible alternatives such as braille or digital texts is essential. This modification ensures she can access the curriculum effectively.

QUESTION 230

Answer: C

Explanation: To ensure James's access to the classroom, the most appropriate action is to install a ramp or lift to make the classroom on the second floor accessible, promoting inclusion and equal access.

QUESTION 231

Answer: C

Explanation: To address Emma's disruptive behavior and maintain a positive learning environment, it is crucial to collaborate with specialists to identify and address the underlying causes, leading to more effective intervention and support.

QUESTION 232

Answer: C

Explanation: Effective instruction for visually impaired students requires tailoring methods to each student's unique needs rather than relying solely on traditional approaches.

QUESTION 233

Answer: B

Explanation: To support the student's access to technology, offering training on screen readers or other assistive technologies can be a helpful solution.

QUESTION 234

Answer: C

Explanation: Adapting instructional resources is done to ensure that students with visual impairments have equal access to educational materials and can participate fully in learning.

QUESTION 235

Answer: C

Explanation: Adaptive and assistive technologies should be selected based on the individual needs of the student with a visual impairment, ensuring a tailored and effective solution.

QUESTION 236

Answer: C

Explanation: To meet the student's preference while ensuring access to materials, exploring options to provide both printed and braille materials can be a solution.

QUESTION 237

Answer: B

Explanation: Ongoing evaluation is important to ensure that adaptive and assistive technologies continue to meet the student's needs and remain effective over time.

QUESTION 238

Answer: C

Explanation: The ultimate goal of adapting instructional methods is to maximize the student's access to instruction and foster their learning, tailoring approaches to their specific needs.

QUESTION 239

Answer: C

Explanation: To ensure effective instruction for Emily in science, it is essential to collaborate with specialists to adapt science materials into accessible formats, allowing her to pursue her interest while receiving accessible content.

QUESTION 240

Answer: D

Explanation: To address John's challenges, it is important to collaborate with website developers to improve accessibility, ensuring that he can access digital content effectively.

QUESTION 241

Answer: C

Explanation: To support Sophia's career aspirations, establishing connections with local music production studios and exploring training opportunities is crucial when the school lacks resources in that area. This facilitates her transition to a music production career.

QUESTION 242

Answer: B

Explanation: The history and philosophy of special education regarding students with visual impairments aim to ensure that visually impaired students receive equal educational opportunities.

QUESTION 243

Answer: C

Explanation: The integration of visually impaired students into mainstream schools marked a turning point toward inclusion and accessible education.

108

QUESTION 244

Answer: B

Explanation: The lack of access to and availability of assistive technology is a key issue that has gained significant attention in recent years in the education of visually impaired students.

QUESTION 245

Answer: C

Explanation: Advancements in technology have led to a significant trend in the growth of digital accessibility and the use of e-books in the education of visually impaired students.

QUESTION 246

Answer: C

Explanation: Research is crucial in the field of education for visually impaired students to identify effective strategies and interventions that can improve outcomes and support their unique needs.

QUESTION 247

Answer: C

Explanation: Recent research has focused on exploring the use of inclusive practices and improving access to curriculum for visually impaired students to enhance their learning experiences.

QUESTION 248

Answer: B

Explanation: One key challenge in conducting research in this field is the limited access to research funding and resources, which can hinder the advancement of knowledge and evidence-based practices for visually impaired students.

QUESTION 249

Answer: A

Explanation: Visually impaired students may struggle with accessing visual materials, such as charts, graphs, or images, which are commonly used in mainstream classrooms. This can hinder their ability to fully participate in lessons.

QUESTION 250

Answer: A

Explanation: It is crucial for teachers to embrace inclusive teaching methods that consider both the cultural backgrounds and visual impairments of their students. This helps create an environment where all students can thrive.

QUESTION 251

Answer: A

Explanation: For visually impaired students, providing a tactile representation of the artwork allows them to explore and understand the piece through touch, providing a meaningful learning experience.

QUESTION 252

Answer: A

Explanation: Visually impaired students may struggle with smoothly tracking lines of text due to their limited visual field. This can affect their reading fluency and comprehension.

QUESTION 253

Answer: A

Explanation: To support a visually impaired student who is also an English language learner, it is important to offer a variety of instructional materials that cater to different learning modalities, including tactile and auditory resources, in addition to language instruction. This helps create a more inclusive and effective learning environment.

QUESTION 254

Answer: C

Explanation: The pupil adjusts in size to control the amount of light entering the eye, ensuring optimal visual clarity. This mechanism is especially important for individuals with visual impairments.

QUESTION 255

Answer: C

Explanation: The retina contains photoreceptor cells that convert incoming light into electrical signals, which are then transmitted to the brain for visual processing.

QUESTION 256

Answer: D

Explanation: Retinitis pigmentosa is a visual impairment that primarily affects the peripheral vision, leading to tunnel vision as central vision deteriorates.

QUESTION 257

Answer: C

Explanation: Cataracts result in a clouding of the eye's lens, which impairs the passage of light and causes blurred vision. This condition can affect individuals with visual impairments.

QUESTION 258

Answer: A

Explanation: High-contrast materials can be beneficial for students with low vision, as they make it easier to distinguish and interpret visual information.

QUESTION 259

Answer: C

Explanation: Orientation and mobility training aims to empower visually impaired students with the skills and confidence to navigate their surroundings independently.

QUESTION 260

Answer: B

Explanation: Braille is a tactile writing system that uses raised dots to represent letters and characters, enabling visually impaired individuals to read and write.

QUESTION 261

Answer: B

Explanation: Magnification is a key optical principle used to enlarge text or images, making them more accessible for individuals with low vision.

QUESTION 262

Answer: A

Explanation: Telescopes are low vision aids that provide magnification for distant objects, making them useful for activities like viewing presentations or lectures in a classroom setting.

QUESTION 263

Answer: A

Explanation: Absorptive filters are designed to reduce glare and enhance contrast, making them an effective solution for individuals who experience discomfort or difficulty due to bright lights.

QUESTION 264

Answer: C

Explanation: A video magnifier (CCTV) provides hands-free magnification, allowing the student to simultaneously use both hands for tasks like writing or referencing a textbook.

QUESTION 265

Answer: A

Explanation: Field of view refers to the area that can be seen through a magnifying device. It's important to consider alongside magnification to ensure that the student can view a sufficient portion of the material.

QUESTION 266

Answer: A

Explanation: A handheld magnifier is a portable low vision aid that can be easily carried and used for reading books or other materials on the go.

QUESTION 267

Answer: A

Explanation: For outdoor activities, especially those in varying weather conditions, having a low vision aid that is weather-resistant is crucial to ensure it remains functional and reliable during outdoor pursuits like birdwatching.

QUESTION 268

Answer: A

Explanation: An IRI is a type of informal assessment that provides detailed information about a student's reading abilities, including comprehension, fluency, and word recognition. It is particularly useful for tailoring instruction to a visually impaired student's specific needs.

QUESTION 269

Answer: A

Explanation: CBM is an ongoing assessment tool that measures a student's progress in specific academic areas, such as mathematics. It provides valuable information for tracking improvements over time.

QUESTION 270

Answer: A

Explanation: Performance-based assessments allow students to demonstrate their knowledge and skills in real-world contexts. This type of assessment is particularly effective for evaluating practical problem-solving abilities, which may not be accurately reflected in written tests.

QUESTION 271

Answer: A

Explanation: It is important to differentiate between factors related to visual impairment and other factors that may influence a student's performance. This ensures a comprehensive and accurate interpretation of assessment results.

QUESTION 272

Answer: A

Explanation: Technology-based assessment tools can be designed with accessibility features, such as screen readers or enlarged text, which can greatly benefit visually impaired students, ensuring they can participate in assessments effectively.

QUESTION 273

Answer: A

Explanation: A portfolio assessment allows the student to showcase a collection of their work, including hands-on experiments, visual representations, and written reflections. This approach provides a more holistic view of their understanding and skills.

QUESTION 274

Answer: A

Explanation: It is important to offer concrete examples to parents, highlighting their child's accomplishments and areas where they may benefit from additional support or accommodations. This approach fosters a constructive and collaborative relationship between parents and educators.

QUESTION 275

Answer: A

Explanation: In this case, using Curriculum-Based Measurement (CBM) would be the most effective approach. CBM involves monitoring a student's progress in specific academic areas over time. It is particularly useful when getting to know a new student's abilities and tailoring instruction to their needs.

QUESTION 276

Answer: A

Explanation: Given Michael's proficiency in hands-on science experiments, a performance-based assessment would be the most appropriate choice. This type of assessment allows him to demonstrate his understanding in a practical, hands-on manner, providing a more accurate reflection of his true abilities.

QUESTION 277

Answer: A

Explanation: An Informal Reading Inventory (IRI) is a valuable tool for ongoing assessment of reading skills. It provides detailed information about a student's reading abilities, allowing the teacher to track Alex's progress and make informed instructional decisions. This is particularly important for a visually impaired student like Alex who may have specific reading needs.

QUESTION 278

Answer: A

Explanation: Culturally responsive teaching practices acknowledge and respect the diverse cultural and linguistic backgrounds of students, including those who are visually impaired. This fosters an inclusive and supportive learning environment.

QUESTION 279

Answer: A

Explanation: Encouraging peer collaboration provides opportunities for the visually impaired student to build positive relationships and receive support from their classmates, which can significantly impact their self-esteem.

QUESTION 280

Answer: A

Explanation: Providing materials in accessible formats is a proactive measure to ensure that visually impaired students have equal access to educational materials. This demonstrates a commitment to meeting their unique needs.

QUESTION 281

Answer: A

Explanation: Fostering a sense of belonging and inclusivity helps students, including visually impaired students, feel valued and supported in their learning environment. This positive atmosphere can significantly impact their attitudes toward learning.

QUESTION 282

Answer: A

Explanation: Actively incorporating diverse perspectives and materials into the curriculum demonstrates an inclusive approach that recognizes and respects the cultural and linguistic differences of visually impaired students, creating a more enriching learning experience.

QUESTION 283

Answer: A

Explanation: Encouraging the student to participate in activities that highlight their strengths and talents can boost their self-esteem and confidence, helping them recognize their capabilities beyond their visual impairment.

QUESTION 284

Answer: A

Explanation: Clear and consistent communication is essential for ensuring that all students, including those who are visually impaired, can effectively access and engage with the learning materials and activities in the classroom. This helps establish a smoothly functioning learning environment.

QUESTION 285

Answer: A

Explanation: Providing materials in accessible formats is crucial for Maria's participation. Additionally, incorporating elements of her cultural background into lessons shows respect for her identity and helps create an inclusive learning environment.

QUESTION 286

Answer: A

Explanation: Leveraging John's interest in technology can significantly enhance his learning experience. Providing access to assistive technology tools tailored to his needs empowers him to utilize digital resources effectively.

QUESTION 287

Answer: A

Explanation: Creating a supportive learning environment for Raj involves fostering a culture of acceptance and celebration of diversity. Recognizing and valuing each student's unique strengths, including those with visual impairments, can positively impact Raj's self-esteem.

QUESTION 288

Answer: A

Explanation: Conducting a braille assessment is the first step to understanding Jane's current level of braille proficiency. This assessment will inform the teacher's approach in tailoring instruction to meet Jane's specific needs.

QUESTION 289

Answer: A

Explanation: Given David's proficiency in using technology, providing training in keyboarding skills and accessible technology options is an effective strategy to enhance his expressive and receptive language abilities.

QUESTION 290

Answer: A

Explanation: Given Emily's interest, providing instruction in Nemeth code and offering challenging math materials will help foster her proficiency in advanced math concepts.

QUESTION 291

Answer: A

Explanation: Encouraging students to actively engage in writing activities using braille promotes their expressive language development and proficiency in using braille as a means of communication.

QUESTION 292

Answer: A

Explanation: To support Sarah's preference and enhance her learning experience, providing access to a refreshable braille display and offering instruction on its use is essential.

QUESTION 293

Answer: A

Explanation: Providing additional braille instruction and offering a variety of materials tailored to Tom's interests can help address his challenges and support his braille literacy development.

QUESTION 294

Answer: A

Explanation: Recognizing and respecting diverse learning styles and preferences involves offering a range of communication options, which may include braille, auditory methods, and technology, to effectively address the needs of visually impaired students.

QUESTION 295

Answer: A

Explanation: Conducting a comprehensive assessment will help pinpoint the specific areas where Alex is facing challenges. This information allows the teacher to customize instruction to address his unique needs, thereby supporting his braille literacy development.

QUESTION 296

Answer: A

Explanation: Given Emily's interest, providing dedicated instruction in the Nemeth code and offering challenging math materials tailored to her abilities and interests will support her in accessing advanced math content.

114

QUESTION 297

Answer: A

Explanation: To best accommodate James's learning preferences, it is important to ensure he has consistent access to a refreshable braille display. Additionally, providing guidance on how to effectively use the device will optimize his learning experience and support his braille literacy development.

QUESTION 298

Answer: A

Explanation: Providing structured social activities with inclusive games and cooperative tasks creates a supportive environment for Emma to practice social interactions, develop social skills, and build friendships with her peers.

QUESTION 299

Answer: A

Explanation: Providing access to technologies with features that support communication and social interactions helps visually impaired students engage with peers and develop important social/emotional skills.

QUESTION 300

Answer: A

Explanation: Implementing strategies for emotional regulation, along with providing creative outlets like art or journaling, allows Jake to express his feelings in a constructive manner and develop essential social/emotional skills.

QUESTION 301

Answer: A

Explanation: Recognizing and considering the individual strengths, challenges, and preferences of visually impaired students is crucial for tailoring instructional methods that effectively support their social/emotional development.

QUESTION 302

Answer: A

Explanation: Fostering a supportive and inclusive environment encourages understanding, empathy, and open communication among all students, which can help overcome potential barriers to social/emotional development for visually impaired students.

QUESTION 303

Answer: A

Explanation: Providing encouragement, facilitating discussions about Lily's interests, and exploring accommodations or modifications are proactive steps to support her in participating in extracurricular activities, which can greatly contribute to her social/emotional development.

QUESTION 304

Answer: A

Explanation: It is crucial to select adaptive and assistive technologies based on individual needs and preferences, and to provide proper training and support to ensure effective use for social/emotional development in visually impaired students. This approach maximizes the benefits of the technologies.

QUESTION 305

Answer: A

Explanation: Facilitating small group activities encourages interaction, teamwork, and collaboration among students. Ensuring Oliver's active participation in such activities can help him build connections with classmates and support his social/emotional development.

QUESTION 306

Answer: A

Explanation: Providing accessible materials in formats like braille or large print addresses Sophie's immediate needs. Additionally, offering encouragement and support will help boost her confidence, addressing her social/emotional well-being.

QUESTION 307

Answer: A

Explanation: Collaborating with relevant stakeholders to ensure accessibility of extracurricular activities is crucial. Providing encouragement and reassurance will help Lucas feel supported and confident in his participation, thereby promoting his social/emotional development.

QUESTION 308

Answer: A

Explanation: Actively listening, validating feelings, and collaborating with the parent are crucial steps in providing meaningful support. This approach fosters trust, open communication, and a collaborative partnership in addressing the child's needs.

QUESTION 309

Answer: A

Explanation: Providing information, orientation opportunities, and facilitating communication with relevant staff members helps ease the transition process for the family and ensures they are well-informed and supported during this important change.

QUESTION 310

Answer: A

Explanation: Offering a safe and empathetic space allows families to express their feelings and concerns. Providing resources or referrals when needed shows that the teacher is there to support the family's emotional well-being in addition to practical matters.

QUESTION 311

Answer: A

Explanation: Providing information on available support networks and resources, and offering assistance in connecting with them, empowers Mark to access valuable resources that can provide additional support and information.

QUESTION 312

Answer: A

Explanation: Offering a meeting provides a personalized opportunity to address Lisa's concerns. Providing information on available resources and services, along with guiding her through the transition process, offers practical support during this important transition.

QUESTION 313

Answer: A

Explanation: Providing a safe and empathetic space allows John to express his feelings and concerns. Offering resources or referrals when needed shows that the teacher is there to support John's emotional well-being in addition to academic matters.

QUESTION 314

Answer: A

Explanation: Providing information on available support networks and resources empowers Mike to access valuable support from other families facing similar challenges. Offering assistance in connecting with them reinforces the teacher's commitment to Mike's well-being and support.

QUESTION 315

Answer: A

Explanation: When faced with conflicting research findings, it is crucial to critically evaluate the quality and source of the research. Considering contextual factors and seeking guidance from experts helps in making informed instructional decisions tailored to the specific needs of visually impaired students.

QUESTION 316

Answer: A

Explanation: Recognizing the diversity among visually impaired students is crucial. Research findings should be applied with the understanding that individualized approaches to instruction are necessary to meet the unique needs of each student.

QUESTION 317

Answer: A

Explanation: Piloting the new method and closely monitoring its effectiveness allows the teacher to assess its suitability for visually impaired students. Adjustments based on ongoing assessment ensure that the method is tailored to their specific needs.

QUESTION 318

Answer: A

Explanation: Applying research findings requires that the research is current and relevant to the specific needs and characteristics of visually impaired students. This ensures that instructional practices are well-suited to their unique requirements.

QUESTION 319

Answer: A

Explanation: When faced with conflicting research findings, it is important to consider the specific needs and preferences of the visually impaired students. Seeking input from relevant stakeholders and carefully weighing the potential benefits and challenges of inclusive education are crucial steps in making informed instructional decisions.

QUESTION 320

Answer: A

Explanation: Ongoing professional development is crucial for teachers to stay updated with current research findings and gain new skills. This enables them to effectively implement research-based practices tailored to the needs of visually impaired students.

QUESTION 321

Answer: A

Explanation: Integrating assistive technology requires a thoughtful approach. Exploring the specific needs and preferences of each student, assessing the appropriateness of available technologies, and providing training and support are crucial steps in ensuring effective use for visually impaired students.

QUESTION 322

Answer: A

Explanation: Spatial reasoning involves understanding and mentally manipulating spatial relationships. It is crucial for developing orientation and mobility skills, enabling visually impaired students to navigate their surroundings safely and independently.

QUESTION 323

Answer: B

Explanation: Tactile perception, or the ability to interpret tactile (touch) information accurately, is essential for proficient braille reading. Students need to develop sensitive touch and discrimination skills to feel and distinguish braille characters effectively.

QUESTION 324

Answer: C

Explanation: Metacognition, or the ability to think about one's thinking and problem-solving processes, is crucial for visually impaired students to adapt and find solutions in diverse situations where visual cues may be limited or unavailable.

QUESTION 325

Answer: C

Explanation: Executive functioning skills, which include organization, planning, and task initiation, are essential for effective writing. These skills help students structure their thoughts and manage the writing process more efficiently, regardless of their visual impairment.

QUESTION 326

Answer: B

Explanation: It is crucial to adapt assessments to ensure they are accessible to visually impaired students. This may involve providing alternative formats, assistive technology, or modifications to the assessment process while maintaining the assessment's integrity.

QUESTION 327

Answer: B

Explanation: Early assessment and intervention for visually impaired students aim to identify their unique needs and provide specialized instruction and support to promote their educational success within inclusive settings.

QUESTION 328

Answer: B

Explanation: If a visually impaired student continues to struggle with assessments, it's important to explore alternative instructional methods tailored to their specific needs, such as tactile or auditory approaches, in addition to accommodations.

QUESTION 329

Answer: C

Explanation: Standardized assessments should be adapted to accommodate the sensory needs of visually impaired students to ensure a fair and accurate assessment of their abilities.

QUESTION 330

Answer: D

Explanation: Assessment in this context is primarily aimed at identifying the specific learning needs of the visually impaired student, which will inform the development of appropriate instructional strategies and interventions.

QUESTION 331

Answer: B

Explanation: Nondiscriminatory and culturally fair assessments are important to provide visually impaired students with equitable opportunities for academic success by eliminating bias and ensuring fairness in the assessment process.

QUESTION 332

Answer: C

Explanation: Advocating for accessible braille versions of assessments is essential to ensure that visually impaired students have the same opportunities as their peers to demonstrate their knowledge and abilities through standardized assessments.

QUESTION 333

Answer: B

Explanation: The special education teacher often takes on the role of coordinating and leading IEP team meetings, ensuring that the student's unique needs and goals are addressed effectively.

QUESTION 334

Answer: B

Explanation: The school psychologist plays a crucial role in conducting assessments to evaluate the student's cognitive and emotional strengths and needs, which inform the development of the IEP.

QUESTION 335

Answer: D

Explanation: The IEP team should prioritize placing the visually impaired student in the least restrictive environment (LRE) that is appropriate for their needs, as mandated by special education law. This decision should be based on a comprehensive evaluation of the student's needs and abilities.

QUESTION 336

Answer: B

Explanation: The primary role of the speech-language pathologist (SLP) on an IEP team is to address the communication and language goals of the student, which can be particularly important for visually impaired students who may have unique communication needs.

QUESTION 337

Answer: B

Explanation: When a visually impaired student changes school districts, it is essential to conduct a new evaluation to assess the student's current strengths and needs, ensuring that the IEP is based on up-to-date information.

QUESTION 338

Answer: C

Explanation: The PLOP section of an IEP provides a description of the student's current academic and functional abilities, serving as the foundation for setting appropriate goals and determining needed supports and accommodations.

QUESTION 339

Answer: C

Explanation: The key guiding principle in determining placement for a visually impaired student should always be the best interests and unique needs of the student. This decision should prioritize the student's educational and developmental goals.

QUESTION 340

Answer: C

Explanation: In this situation, the IEP team should conduct a comprehensive evaluation to assess Sarah's strengths and needs, ensuring that the placement decision is based on her individual requirements rather than solely on the parents' or principal's preferences.

QUESTION 341

Answer: C

Explanation: It is important to consider the parent's concerns while developing an IEP. The team should work collaboratively to find a mutually acceptable solution that balances Alex's therapy needs with his academic progress.

QUESTION 342

Answer: C

Explanation: To ensure that Emily's new IEP accurately reflects her current abilities and needs, the IEP team should conduct a comprehensive evaluation. Relying solely on the old IEP may not address her current educational requirements effectively.

QUESTION 343

Answer: B

Explanation: Before selecting instructional methods or assistive technologies, it is essential to assess Mark's current skills and needs comprehensively. This assessment will provide a clear understanding of where he needs support and guide the selection of appropriate strategies.

QUESTION 344

Answer: C

Explanation: The selection of adaptive or assistive technologies for orientation and mobility training should always be based on the individual needs and preferences of the visually impaired student. Technology should align with the student's goals and abilities.

QUESTION 345

Answer: B

Explanation: It is important to conduct a thorough assessment to determine whether a guide dog is a suitable option for Sarah based on her specific needs, abilities, and preferences. The decision should prioritize her best interests.

QUESTION 346

Answer: A

Explanation: The student's preference and comfort with tactile learning materials are important factors to consider when adapting instructional methods for teaching orientation and mobility skills. Tailoring instruction to the student's preferences can enhance engagement and learning outcomes.

QUESTION 347

Answer: C

Explanation: To support John's request, it is essential to assess his readiness and provide him with appropriate training on using the smartphone app. This approach allows for the integration of technology into his orientation and mobility skills as long as it aligns with his goals and abilities.

QUESTION 348

Answer: B

Explanation: When teaching orientation and mobility skills to a visually impaired student with additional disabilities, it is crucial to incorporate multisensory and individualized instructional methods to accommodate their unique needs and enhance their learning experience.

QUESTION 349

Answer: C

Explanation: It is essential to assess Maria's physical abilities and explore alternative mobility aids that may be better suited to her needs and comfort. This approach ensures that she receives appropriate orientation and mobility training that aligns with her capabilities.

QUESTION 350

Answer: C

Explanation: In this scenario, collaborating with a physical therapist is crucial to address David's physical challenges. This collaboration can help develop strategies and adaptations tailored to his specific mobility needs, ensuring that he can participate in orientation and mobility training effectively.

QUESTION 351

Answer: C

Explanation: To support Sarah's request, it is essential to assess her readiness and provide her with appropriate training on using the smartphone app. This approach allows for the integration of technology into her orientation and mobility skills as long as it aligns with her goals and abilities.

QUESTION 352

Answer: C

Explanation: It is important to assess James's goals and provide comprehensive training on using the white cane if it aligns with his needs and preferences. This approach allows James to explore different mobility options and make informed choices about his orientation and mobility methods.

QUESTION 353

Answer: C

Explanation: To effectively evaluate and select assistive technologies, it is crucial to conduct a comprehensive assessment of Alex's individual needs, preferences, and abilities. This assessment will help tailor the technology to best support his learning.

QUESTION 354

Answer: D

Explanation: When adapting instructional methods for a visually impaired student with multiple disabilities, individualization is essential. Instruction should be tailored to the unique needs and abilities of the student, which may include a combination of tactile, auditory, and other approaches.

QUESTION 355

Answer: C

Explanation: To support Sarah's request, it is essential to assess her readiness and provide her with appropriate training on using the smartphone app. This approach allows for the integration of technology into her learning if it aligns with her goals and abilities.

QUESTION 356

Answer: D

Explanation: The primary consideration when selecting adaptive or assistive technologies should be their alignment with the student's individualized educational goals and needs. Technology should support and enhance the achievement of those goals.

QUESTION 357

Answer: C

Explanation: To support James's request, it is essential to assess his goals and provide him with comprehensive guide dog training if it aligns with his needs and preferences. This approach allows James to explore different mobility options and make informed choices about his individualized instruction.

Milton Keynes UK
Ingram Content Group UK Ltd.
UKHW030629161023
430697UK00014B/601